Women in Ministry

In the same series

edited by John Martin
Curate's Egg. The inside story of what a curate's life is really like

Women in Ministry

Edited by

Susan Penfold

HIGHLAND BOOKS

ISBN: 0 946616 81 7

Cover illustration: Taffy Davies

Printed in Great Britain for
HIGHLAND BOOKS
Broadway House, The Broadway
Crowborough, East Sussex TN6 1HQ
by Clays Ltd, St Ives plc
Typeset by Rowland Phototypesetting Ltd,
Bury St Edmunds, Suffolk

Contents

Introduction

There is a widespread caricature of church life which sees the whole show as being kept on the road by an army of middle-aged women (preferably wearing hats) busily engaged in cleaning, arranging flowers, organising jumble sales, polishing the brass and making tea; while the vicar or minister (male, of course) seems to operate in a totally different sphere. I'm not sure that was ever a realistic picture of church life—it certainly isn't today. For one thing 'lay' people are increasingly being seen to have responsibility for the whole of church life, spiritual as well as practical matters; though I'm not sure how new that is—many of those gallant be-hatted ladies of the caricature operated a powerful network of pastoral care. And when it comes to 'the minister' the traditional division between male and female is gradually breaking down.

I wrote to a friend for help in finding potential contributors to this book, and she replied, 'I hope the book isn't just going to feature "ordained" women in the Anglican sense of the word—because women's gifts and ministries are far broader than that.' I would want to affirm that most strongly. Nevertheless, I decided to confine myself broadly to women working in what is sometimes called 'professional ministry', because I wanted to build up a picture of what women are doing in what has been traditionally a man's world (indeed one of the few areas left as potentially a continuing male preserve by the Sex Discrimination Act).

Most women ministers have had the experience of encountering people who have hesitations about accepting their ministry, simply because they have never seen a woman minister in action before. They are often pleasantly surprised by the experience! I wanted to produce a book which would help more people to see that women in ministry are not strange beings from outer space, but people whom God has called and gifted, and chooses to use in his service (despite all our imperfections!).

I would like to thank many people who have helped with this book: Edward England, for suggesting and backing the idea; my various friends and acquaintances, for their help in suggesting possible contributors, especially Di Lammas of the Church Pastoral Aid Society; and most of all the contributors—it would have been a pretty dull book without them!

Susan Penfold

1

Getting on with the Job

by

Mavis Bexon

Mavis Bexon is an Anglican deacon planting a church on the Oakwood Estate in Derby

The inside of Derby Cathedral is not beautiful with its liberal supply of gilt paint, dazzling chandeliers and glossy black painted wrought iron. There are no mellow stone walls or graceful lines leading to focal points. Of the five hymns we sang four were unknown to the fifteen women ordained deacon. I did not know any of them but nothing could have taken away from the excitement of that day, 26th April 1987. Some were in cassock-albs while others wore surplice and cassock. Some wore 'dog collars' and others chose not to. We laughed as we saw each other dressed up.

We were aware of being part of history being made that day. In some ways the wrong done to humanity through the Sex Discrimination Act was being righted, or partly. The church's exemption from the Act had done a great disservice to Christianity. Jesus had spent thirty years bringing God down to earth and earth had managed to put him back on a plane where his followers were not subject to the rules of the rest of the human race.

The bishop, cathedral staff, friends and relatives were all as excited as we were. Whatever debates were going on outside, here was a cathedral of people affirming our ministry and rejoicing over the recognition the church was giving to us. For that is what it meant to me. In what other profession would qualified people be classified as 'lay'? I was now recognised by the church as one of its ministers. It did not affect the way I thought about myself. I had been ministering for years, first licensed 'lady worker', then 'parish worker', then ordained 'deaconess'. But who knew what a lady worker, parish worker or deaconess was? Everybody knows a 'Reverend' is a minister of the Christian church. The only thing I wanted was the freedom to get on with the job I had been given to do, and an important part of that freedom was recognition by the church at large. The bishop prayed for us, '. . . give to these your servants grace and power to fulfil their ministry . . . having full assurance of faith, abounding in hope and being rooted and grounded in love. . . .'

After the ordination we went into the vestry to receive official documents. The Bishop of Derby was Cyril Bowles (since retired) and he said he and his legal advisers had looked very thoroughly into what they could put on my licence. 'I would like to make it "priest-in-charge",' he said, 'but the nearest I can get is "deacon-in-charge of the Church on Oakwood".' We were still held back because we were deacons but not priests. In the Church of England that meant we could not take communion, be an incumbent or a bishop.

We were told we should read an assent to the Thirty-Nine Articles and authority of the bishop before a priest that evening or the next Sunday. That was a problem. We were experienced ministers, unlike the men who were ordained straight from college, and were not taking services alongside priests. We each had to make special arrangements for a priest to hear our assent, perhaps at the beginning or end of a service. I read mine before a congregation which met in my home on the Oakwood Estate in Derby, a new development which was going to be the biggest private housing complex in Europe, we were told.

I had gone there to 'plant' a church, and a group of Christians had quickly come together. First of all we met for prayer and Bible study, then we had our first service of public worship at Pentecost 1986. Helping to plant or establish an indigenous church seemed to have become my lot for the last twenty-five years and yet I had come to it in a roundabout way. Never one to plan ahead, it seems that God has pushed me from one thing to another.

It started I suppose when I was sitting in the staff-room of the public library where I was working after training at Loughborough College (now a university). I was having a tea break and questions were going round and round in my mind. I had been reading lots of missionary books, especially those published by the Overseas Missionary Fellowship. I was already doing a lot of voluntary work in my local church but felt I should do more. I was healthy and free and I really wanted to know whether God wanted me to be a full-time missionary. My feet were propped up on the table and I lazily took an ever-present Bible out of my handbag. Surely the answer should be there somewhere?

I was in the process of reading the Bible in the same way as any other book, from cover to cover, the way we were always told not to read it! But I had done this for years, ending at Revelation 22 and starting again at Genesis 1. On this occasion I was up to Numbers 32. It was about the tribes of Reuben and Gad who had a lot of livestock. When they saw how suitable the land of Jazer and Gilead was for cattle they asked Moses if they could remain there rather than crossing the Jordan and fighting for land on the other side. Moses explained that if they did not all go into the fight together none of them would possess the promised land.

Was this God talking to me? If I did not leave the comfort of home to join the fight to conquer the Far East for Christ, did it mean that there were those who would not become Christians because of my complacency? I looked again at the Authorised Version I was reading at the time, 'Why sit ye here while your brethren go to war?' That was it. My feet came off the table. I could not wait to get things in motion to propel me into this missionary adventure.

It meant training and I went to Redcliffe, an inter-denominational college in Chiswick, London. Nearing the end of the course I applied to OMF and was not accepted. This was a blow and I did not know what to do next, but I had arranged to do voluntary work in my home church for three months, the time I had calculated to have free before going on, as I thought, to language study. The three months stretched to eleven and it was during this time that I realised God was calling me to be a missionary in my own country. It was not until some time later that I took in the rest of the story of Reuben and Gad. Moses had said that if they would join the battle to get the promised land they could return to the pasture they had claimed for their cattle. And in Joshua 12 this happened.

The Church of England now required me to do their training after I had been recommended by the selection conference. As they were going to pay my wages that seemed quite reasonable, but it was with impatience that I entered St Michael's College, Oxford.

In the months between church work and St Michael's I had worked for five weeks in a toy shop, three months in a factory and a further three months as a home help. I would like to say I had worked this out deliberately to gain experience but in fact it just happened. I did not have a grant to go to Redcliffe and had been glad to return to the library at the end of each term to earn some money. But when I tried to get back after the church work I could no longer be considered a student and would therefore have to repay the superannuation I had withdrawn and spent. As Christmas was coming up I saw the temporary job advertised in the toy shop and after Christmas the only employment freely available seemed to be in factories, so I took a job packing up orders for shops, intending this should last me until my third college. But, having missed the early morning factory bus for the third time in a week, I wandered down into the town of Nottingham, passing the home help office on the way. I retraced my steps, then walked backwards and forwards several times before going inside and coming out a little later with green overalls, kneeling mat and rubber gloves. These months of working with different kinds of people in situations I had been unused to proved to be good experience. I made some good friends through the home help service and I was asked to stay on as supervisor. But, no, on I went to my final college.

I only had to do one year as the two years at Redcliffe had been taken into consideration. The time was spent mostly on subjects specifically related to Anglicanism. St Mike's later joined with Dalton House and they both became part of Trinity College, Bristol, where men and women began to train together.

I was looking forward to my first appointment which was in Carlton, Nottinghamshire. This was the county I had originally come from, but I was some miles from home in an area previously unknown to me. My father had died when I was twenty, but my mother, brother and three sisters were all at my licensing and glad, I am sure, that I at last had a proper job again!

I lived in a couple of rooms on the first floor of the rectory. An all-purpose room acted as kitchen, dining-room, sitting-room and study. A small bedroom led off and I shared a bathroom down the corridor with another lodger who worked for the Church Pastoral Aid Society. We had fields on three sides of us and mice were regular visitors. They would crawl over my bed during the night sometimes and once interrupted a Sunday school teachers' meeting by making a racket running across the shelves in the cooker. It became part of the curate's daily routine to inspect the trap, for once I had found a dead mouse in it I never had the courage to look again.

St Paul's, Carlton, had mixed housing, old and new, detached and terraced. There was also a council estate a mile or two away from the parish church. The rector felt it needed special attention, and a mission hall had been built a year or so before I arrived. A work had been started and I was asked to follow it up. So began my work in an urban area, the type God was going to keep me in for the next twenty years and more.

There were three of us on the staff and we worked long hours. The day began with prayers in a cold, dark church. While other people were making whoopee in the sixties, Christian workers seemed to think one prayer before breakfast was worth ten after it. I have never been at my best first thing in the morning and one day when I staggered down the vestry steps and fell through the door, I said, 'It's foggy outside.' One look at my face and the obvious reply came, 'It's foggy inside.'

But that was with my colleagues. I was a different person around the parish, fitting into the role I felt was expected of me. The journey from the rectory to the estate was uphill all the way. Freewheeling back was easy on my push-bike, but the half-hour ride up was something to be endured rather than enjoyed. Not that I would let it show, for I had a fixed smile all the way up, showing what a happy little ambassador for Christ I was, so that everybody would know I could be counted on to give spiritual help to all those who needed it.

I suppose the rector was ahead of his time because he had no discrimination against women and I did all the law would allow. I was responsible for the services at the mission hall and the many activities that went on during the week. I had great backing from the small group of worshippers already gathered and we did a lot of outreach with more enthusiasm than know-how. I was hindered by not living on the estate but in those days the church did not consider housing for women, nor were we provided with telephones. The wages were low (£450 a year) and I was so poor after all those colleges that I could not do anything about it myself. We were also held back by being a mission of St Paul's. Baptisms and communion were held at the parish church and of course we were not licensed for weddings so we did not have the casual contacts you would normally get within the Church of England.

Only one of our members had a car and we used it for everything. My home church had a large cupboard to get rid of and we transferred it to Carlton on the roof-rack, the cupboard coming well over the car at the front and the back. This housed all our equipment for services and Sunday school. Bigger things were kept in the kitchen or the two lavatories. We developed a real affection for this car and it was a day of celebration when the owner had the indicators changed from the kind that plopped out at angles to the car (trafficators) to blinkers.

Our most successful Harvest Supper was in co-operation with the local mobile chip shop. The owner brought the van to our kitchen window and we passed hot plates out to be returned full of fish, chips and peas. It was the fun the Christians had together that flowed over into the community and it attracted more people to the gospel than any direct evangelism did.

I had my first experience of going to court when I was contacted by the probation officer of a lad I knew. He had broken into the gas meter at home for the umpteenth time and the probation officer wondered if I would put in a good word for him at court, which I did. He avoided being 'put away' by my saying I would keep an eye on him, but it was easier said than done as we did not live in the same house and the next time the meter went, so did Stewart. I visited him in the remand centre and felt how inadequate we all were as he stood there, a tall lad of fourteen, in the uniform of short trousers and long blue socks. My heart went out to him but I had experienced nothing in life that equipped me to be of any real help. We lost touch when I moved but I still wonder whether he ever made good.

It was up to Barrow-in-Furness for my next home. Friends from Carlton drove up the bits of furniture I had. Unlike curates, women were not given any removal allowance and I just had enough money to hire the van. A church friend who was a scrap dealer found me chairs and a table, wardrobe and washstand. My mother gave me a bed and the cheque I was given (£15) from Carlton as a leaving present bought two armchairs. I took the piano from home and, as the previous occupier had gone abroad as a missionary and left her carpets behind, I had enough for my needs.

Barrow is a shipbuilding town and the parish of St Mary's mainly consisted of terraced housing. Because their livelihood was largely dependent on the shipyard most people gave their children the best education they could to give them other options. We had a flourishing youth work but most of the people we were involved with went to college or university and never came back.

For two years I was the only woman worker in the diocese and not listed in the Carlisle directory. When I tried to rectify this the editor offered to enter me with the church social workers, and when I said I should be under my parish he flatly refused, saying there was no such thing as a woman minister.

Most of my time in Barrow was spent on the youth work and I had little opportunity for taking part in services until the vicar left and Chris Idle (the curate) and I did the interregnum. It was Chris who got me on the list to receive the bishop's Ad Clerum and later on the deanery list so that I did eventually get invited to deanery events. Prior to that it was as if I did not exist beyond my own parish. Chris also got me and other women in the North West invited to the Eclectics Society. This was a group started by John Stott and friends for young evangelical clergy to help them support each other, at a time when evangelicals were thin on the ground. It was another 'men only' group but the men agreed, at Chris' request, to admit women in ministry as associates. Later they became members in their own right.

I had exchanged my bike for a moped and was able to get to the Lake District on days off, but I was very homesick. I was there for four months before I was free to go home and then only because it was Christmas. For those four months I did not meet anyone I had known before going to Barrow. Later family and friends visited me but it is not a place you pass through, and it took some time for me to get used to the insularity.

My home was the old verger's house, surrounded on three

sides this time by church halls, so it was dark and damp. It opened onto the pavement and I was scared when drunks pounded on my door at night as they passed by. On one occasion the man was more persistent than others and I was terrified until I heard two other men get rid of him. I looked round the curtains and it was an old man and his son-in-law from across the road who were protecting me. I became friendly with them after that and it was Ben and his daughter who helped me to cover the glossy painted walls in my house with wallpaper we had bought in the sales.

Ben became the church caretaker and looked after the vicarage garden. We tried to do something to brighten up my backyard and obtained a barrel from the brewery. Sawed in two, Ben's daughter had one half and I the other. When I was trying to grow things in mine he turned up with a beautiful rose bush but would not admit to there being any connection with the vicar's complaint that he had a rose bush missing from his garden.

Wages were improved and I saved £60 to buy my first car, a 1956 A30. Ben filled it with petrol for my 'maiden voyage'. We donned our best clothes and went out for a run, Ben treating us to a meal into the bargain. The last time I saw him, when I was visiting for the church's centenary, he had had a stroke. But I hope he understood when I tried to tell him how much I had appreciated his friendship, for he died soon afterwards.

Another person I got to know well was Jim who had a brain far in advance of his years. He was therefore bored at school and always looking for ways to exercise his mind. I met him when I was visiting an old lady. He came to her door collecting jumble. With the money he made at the sale he printed literature to launch a new political party. On the manifesto his name was down as leader and the other names were fictitious. He did quite well as an orator, looking older than his sixteen years, but the trouble came when he tried to get elected on to the city council. By then his interest had gone into something else anyway. Christianity was always a subject of interest to him and he was coming round to me regularly to talk about it. He was a funny looking lad, short sighted yet owlish in his National Health spectacles. His nails were bitten and he was never clean. His clothes were usually from jumble sales and had a smell around them of stale tobacco and sweat from their previous owners. He disappeared for a while then came back homeless and the curate (David Gregg had succeeded Chris Idle) put him up as a temporary measure. It was when he stole from the Greggs, including taking money from their children's money boxes, that I really had a good row with Jim and did not hear anything more of him until I was in Liverpool.

I had been almost three years in Carlton and almost five in Barrow and I was to spend seven years in Liverpool, some of the happiest of my career. I had first been attracted to Everton when I visited a college friend who was working there for the Beacon Group of Churches. What had been nine parishes had been put together with Shrewsbury House, a mission of Shrewsbury School, to be worked as a unit by a large team of church and community workers. The area was not large and the church buildings had been close together. It seemed that in the time of Bishop Ryle, as a pub had been put up on one corner of the street a church was built on the other. Terraced houses had been pulled down and there were twenty high-rise blocks, making that more per area than anywhere else in the country.

As I had visited my friend Olivia I passed graffiti announcing in six-foot-high letters, 'Billy is a Bastard' countered by 'Down with the Pope'. It was later I was to learn of the orange (Billy being William of Orange) and green quarrels, the orange being extreme Protestants and the green Roman Catholics. As I got out of the car at the bottom of Olivia's block of flats, I parked where she had told me to so that we could see the car through her window. A boy of seven or eight came up to me. 'Mind yer car, Miss?' he asked. I said, 'No thank you,' but dared him to harm it as his eye met mine. When I repeated the story to Olivia she said it was a protection racket and I should have paid him. I had understood that but nevertheless felt it was right to challenge him and that my car would be all right. It was. When Olivia left I took her place on the team.

Two clergymen were licensed at the same time as I was and there was no difference in the way I was treated to them. That made four clergy and me plus various youth and community workers. As we were all more or less of the same age and experience there was no leader or vicar and the constitution was that we could elect our own leader every September. This lasted until a new parish was formed in 1974. The social needs were enormous and the team had already put into practice suggestions that were to be made in the 'Faith in the City' report in 1985. I went to Everton in 1970 and the group had been going since 1963 so they were well in advance of contemporary thinking and eyed suspiciously by other evangelicals who thought they had gone off the spiritual boil.

My sister, Jean, lived in Cheshire at the time and it was a great help to go over to her the night before my day off and wake up in a different environment. I had chosen to live in a high-rise flat and was glad to do so because I got to know the people of the area very well. But I learned a lesson about specific prayer when I moved in. My sister and her husband had said they would help me to move and I did not think they would be very happy to see me living in the flats, so I prayed that the sun would shine the day we moved in, working on the principle that the sun would make everything look better. I moved on Bank Holiday Monday and the sun poured down. As it was a Bank Holiday the caretakers had not been on duty since Friday afternoon and the rubbish chutes on the landing were overflowing, corridors covered in dog dirt and the lifts full of sick and urine after the Saturday night spree, and the heat of the sun made sure the stench was as pungent as it could be. My brother-in-law never did eat a meal in my flat all the time I lived there.

It was noisy living in the flats as you could hear the occupants above as well as those on each side, and the plumbing left much to be desired. Each time a lavatory was flushed the noise went down the whole of that column. We had a flood for two months when our electricity had to be used carefully and sometimes not at all. The council refused to believe there was a burst pipe somewhere in the top of the block until somebody had the water diagnosed as tap water. The workmen had previously said it was rain water coming in. Once diagnosed, it was put right within an hour. I tried to get those who had suffered to claim compensation for loss of carpets and inconvenience but only one family joined me in this. The rest were just so pleased the flood had stopped they did not look for anything else. They were used to getting the wrong end of a deal.

At one time a prostitute lived just by me and there were times when my door was knocked on by mistake, but my neighbours gave me the same protection as they had in Barrow. I would lie there quaking to hear a voice shout, 'If you don't get away from that door I'll throw you over the balcony.'

It was while I was in Liverpool that I was first invited to Chapter meetings, which had normally been for clergy only, and I was warned by my colleagues that some of the men would not want me there, but I made sure I went and was soon accepted. We still had to be nominated for the Parochial Church Council, unlike the men who were on as a matter of course. For the first time I was also invited to the annual clergy conference. A college had been closed in the Wirral and the money from it had been put into scholarships to give sabbaticals to clergy, at Wycliffe Hall, Oxford. The man in charge of in-service training rang me one day to ask me whether I would be interested in going to Wycliffe. He was going to ask for the constitution of the scholarship to be changed to include women but did not want to do so unless he was sure women would take advantage of it. He had already asked the two most senior women in the diocese and they had each said they would like to go but not be first. One of them had suggested I might blaze the trail so I agreed to go and others have continued to go after me.

I did my first baptism in Liverpool; the baby of a girl who

had been on the Pathfinder camps I used to lead. I had known her since she was sixteen, when I was still in Barrow and Olivia had recommended her to camp with me. But with a large team I did not do a great deal in the services. I was more involved with people on a personal level, though a big project I inherited from Eddie Neale, when he left to go to Radio Merseyside as Religious Adviser, was the pensioners' holiday. This was good fun but very tiring as the holiday-makers were up before breakfast and in bed long after the day had ended in order to get as much enjoyment out of the holiday as they possibly could. One night I was fetched out of bed by some women who thought their friend had had a stroke. But I knew the symptoms by now and recognised the smell. 'She's drunk,' I said. 'Let's get her to bed.' It was a story related year after year, that I the 'innocent' had diagnosed where hardened drinkers had failed. The fact that the hardened drinkers were muddle-headed at the time did not occur to them.

There were spiritual results of a different nature though. Each morning began with Bible reading, a short talk and prayer and some of the older people did come into a new faith. When I led the confirmation class there was a year in which six of the twelve candidates were senior citizens. They joined in discussion with refreshing honesty and one day when we were talking about love and forgiveness a woman volunteered, 'I always hated my husband, even before we were married.'

'Why did you marry him?'

'To spite him,' was the immediate reply.

But Liverpool people do not hold grudges, as I found out when I caught three boys trying to break into the church with a battering ram. Quick as lightning I bashed their heads together and they were so humiliated their suggestions as to what they were going to do with me do not bear recording. But I met them later in the day and they called out with their usual friendship, 'Eyup Mave.' This year, nineteen years after the event, I received a telephone call from one of them. 'I thought you'd like to know,' he said,

'I've become a Christian.' He told me about it in detail and I was so glad. After all those years he knew I would still care enough to be thrilled to bits, and he cared enough to want me to be thrilled.

I cannot give such a happy ending to Jim's story, though it was similar in that he contacted me after a number of years when the last time we had spoken was with harsh words. I received a letter which began, 'You will see I am a guest of Her Majesty the Queen.' Sure enough he was in Walton Prison and had sent me an authorisation for a visit. He did this every month he was imprisoned as none of his family or friends wanted to see him. He was in the protected section as he had allegedly committed homosexual offences against minors as well as forgery. The entrance to his visiting quarters was blocked by a warder sitting at a table. He looked down the big ledger for Jim's name and asked, without looking up, 'Relationship?' I hesitated. 'Shall I put friend?' he offered. I was tempted to say I was a minister of the church and he was nothing to me personally. It seemed a long time before I made a reply but it was probably a split second. 'Yes,' I agreed, 'put friend.' After he was released I tried to help him in his determination to keep away from his old associates. He had returned to Barrow but telephoned me every week for encouragement until the last time. He had returned to his former homosexual partner, the man who had reported him to the police after they had quarrelled and had testified against him at the trial which led to his imprisonment. Jim was very drunk. I never heard from him again.

After Eddie Neale left Radio Merseyside he went to Bestwood, Nottingham, where I joined him six months later. The parish of Bestwood consisted of three council estates at the time. It later took in more and Eddie had gone there to build up a team ministry of which I was the first recruit. Ted Lyons, who had been converted at the Mayflower Family Centre when David Sheppard was the warden was to join a year later. The team built up to five when the parish took in more estates, but there were still only the three of us when we decided the best way to work was for each of us to be responsible for the area and the church where we lived. So I was back where I had started in Carlton with a place of worship I was responsible for. Top Valley was where I lived in a council flat over the dentist and next door to the community centre.

It was in this parish that I took my first funeral service. I visited the widow of the dead man and her brother-in-law was there. 'I do not know whether you understand what this young lady is saying,' he said. 'She is going to take the funeral service.'

'You can't do that,' she informed me.

I told her I could and I would, to which she responded, 'Poor old Bert. Second best in life and second best in death.' They were both to apologise after the funeral and things have changed since this happened in 1977. It would never be queried today.

The church was a dual purpose building and as such left much to be desired. But we had a parish mission which ended in a week of evangelism and many people who had no church background became Christians. I had been called to missionary work in my own country and saw it working out in my home town. This was a tremendous privilege and I realised this even more than ever when I heard that women I had trained with who had gone abroad were denied evangelism. Most of them were in countries where it was forbidden to proselytise. They were doing nursing or teaching or, in one case, housekeeping, whereas I had all the freedom I needed to invite anyone to become a Christian.

After I had been in Top Valley four years the diocese bought a house for me so I had a garden for the first time. I enjoyed this and loved to see things grow, but my enjoyment was spoiled by an irate woman who smashed my windows on two occasions. The person she had been living with had left her and then become a Christian. His new-found faith and friends within the church gave him the strength to lead a new life and keep away from his old haunts. But the woman could not believe it was God who had changed him. She thought it was me and when her endeavours to get him back failed she became my shadow. She was always hoping to catch me with her old boyfriend and stood outside the house for hours. She wrote to my bishop and the press. She jumped on the bonnet of my car one day with a hatchet. I was involved in going to court on my own behalf this time in order to get an injunction against her. I was ready to run away but Eddie wrote some of the story up in the *Church of England Newspaper* one week and said I felt like giving up. I had a letter from a total stranger urging me not to do so and giving me a great deal of encouragement. So I hung on until the tide turned.

From Barrow onwards I have had students on placement and always found this a happy time. In Nottingham we had students from St John's College on six-month placements of four periods (that is half-days) a week. They mostly worked hard and caught the vision of building up the indigenous church. They introduced drama and new music. They often had good ideas and made me think things through afresh. I am still in touch with all but one of them and it is good to see the way their ministries have developed through the years.

Where Liverpool's problems were mostly stealing, Top Valley's were more often of an emotional nature. It took me some time to say 'no' to a person who would ring up at the least convenient time saying that if I did not go to see her she would commit suicide. A wise friend told me to say, 'Then you will just have to do it.' What of the risk? The same friend told me I could not be responsible and she was right. In the end each person is responsible for himself. After nine years in Top Valley I was worn out and yet it was with reluctance that I went to Derby.

The reluctance was in going to a private housing estate. There was no graffiti and nobody sitting on their front doorsteps talking. The gardens and houses were neat and tidy and took a bit of getting used to. After I had first seen the area I wrote to say I would not be working there but the letter didn't get posted. So I wrote again expressing my doubts, at the same time realising that was where I had to go.

It has in fact been very good for me. The Christians who have met together are gifted and committed and reliable. They have made me polish up what is left of my brains after years of talking and thinking in the lowest common denominator. Meeting in my 'front-room', as the press called it, meant we had a very close fellowship.

We had great problems trying to obtain land for a church building and bashed our heads against brick walls very often. But the problems have brought us closer together. When the house was so full that worshippers had to sit on windowsills and the floor, a Roman Catholic convent was bought by the Anglican Order of the Holy Name and they offered us the use of their chapel. This has made such a difference to us. We have room to move about and this year for the first time we are asking the congregation to bring gifts for the Harvest Festival. We never had anywhere to put them before. I still have clubs and the Mothers' and Toddlers' group in my home but it is great to have it free on Sundays. Before we went into the convent we had to move all the furniture out of the sitting-room every weekend and lay out chairs. Sunday school was in the kitchen and I had to check after they had gone to see what setting the washing machine had been moved to and whether the deep freeze was on fast.

Most of the inhabitants are young families and we are geared towards this. There is always somebody in the fellowship pregnant and I say that tomes have been written on church growth but we grow in number just by doing what comes naturally. We get most of our contacts through baptism enquiries and one of our members does all the clerical work connected with this, and also the visiting after the baptism. One of the nuns also visits for us. House groups are growing and there is a general desire to grow more in our Christian faith.

Oakwood is going to be made into a new parish and will be part of a group ministry in which two of the other churches will be urban. I can see Oakwood being a good place of resource for those with fewer advantages. Hopefully (though it still needs to be confirmed) we have a piece of land on which to build. We are also in the process of becoming a local ecumenical project.

Looking back, God has given me many opportunities for service over the years and I am glad I have taken most of them, however imperfectly I have carried out the tasks. I have made mistakes, but did somebody not say that if you do not make a mistake you do not make anything? If nobody did, then somebody should have, so I had better say it now!

2

Discovering a Role

by

Chris Howden

Chris Howden has many responsibilities, including being a voluntary schools worker with Scripture Union, and leading the youth and children's work at Lymm Baptist Church, Cheshire, where her husband Brian is the minister

I was thirty-one years old—a wife and a mother, dissatisfied with my marriage and struggling with the children. I had looked for consolation in work and pleasure but knew the answer was only to be found by asking God to change me! I have met so many people who say, 'I can't help it . . . that's just the way I feel.' I know those feelings are real and valid but I also know that those feelings can be changed, if you want them to be, by the grace and power of God. It was from dying embers that God fanned a flame and restored our marriage, giving us greater joy in our marriage and family than we had ever known. It was through that fire, too, that the voice of God called us to a greater commitment to him, a greater awareness of his power, and a vision for what he wanted to do in the lives of others. We came to see that God was calling us into full-time Christian work.

The call came to us both. We were convinced it was a work God was calling us to share together, and in the course of time the direction seemed to be the pastoral ministry and leadership of a church. The question then was, 'How should we prepare ourselves for this task?'

For Brian, my husband, with a flourishing career in the insurance industry, it meant a completely new start and theological training. For me it wasn't so clear cut. Our children were then aged seven and nine. I had trained as a teacher, teaching religious education, so had some theological background and biblical study behind me, but would have liked to have done some further training. However, we decided to move from Suffolk to London so that we could be near London Bible College where my husband was to train. Our lifestyle was to change dramatically—the executive fast lane had come to an abrupt end—and I felt sure my role at that time was to support us all through this change and to wait for God to guide me as to the future when everything settled down.

Brian commenced his three-year degree course in 1982. The children started new schools and we joined a free church near our new rented home, where I had been a member in my teens. I now waited for God to show me the next step, wondering if he would, afraid of what it might mean for me. Yet God had proved to us in so many ways over the previous two years that he was in control. I remembered back to the time when we were looking for a home in London, with two weeks to go before the end of term. I was worrying about arranging the children's schooling before the schools closed. Nothing was available, let alone at a rent which we could afford, and I started to panic. Brian, however, was convinced we should go on praying for a house for which we would not need to pay rent in August, as we planned to return to Suffolk in the summer. I felt this was foolhardy—I was prepared to pray for anything! It was then that the phone had rung. 'I have been asked to contact you as I have a house to rent,' said a voice. The price was unbelievably low, the exact price we could afford. The accommodation was what we needed and we could have it for three years. There was only one snag: he wished to return to it for the month of August!

This was one of many ways in which God had proved his faithfulness to us—so why was I worried now? It is good that God our Father is so patient with us! Yet once again it became clear that God had a plan for me. 'We've been praying for you to come,' I was told as soon as we settled into our new church. 'We have heard all about you, know you are a teacher and have experience of running a playgroup. We are desperate for a new supervisor; our playgroup will have to close otherwise. You must be the answer to our prayers!' This certainly did seem God's way. I could work in the church and community but still have time for the family and other activities. God had answered everyone's prayers.

So I worked in the church playgroup and attended evening classes at the college. I joined my husband for the pastoral summer schools. We sat up till all hours discussing the various theological issues that he was grappling with and I was pleased I could remember so much of the study I thought I had forgotten from my teacher training. It was a busy time. Brian studied hard, and we worked hard in the church and ran a house group. I once again considered doing a one-year course but still felt it would put us all under so much pressure. I was gaining experience in practical ministry and that seemed, for the time being, to be the right thing to do.

Three years passed. Brian was accepted by the Baptist Union and ordained as a Baptist minister. We were called to work in a Cheshire village, a community of about 12,000 people. 'What does your wife see as her role?' one of the deacons asked as we were being interviewed. It was a good question and one I would be better able to answer now after five years. At that time, I had no pre-conceived ideas but I knew I wanted to work alongside Brian. I did not see myself returning to teaching but being available to work in the church in whatever way God led me. I was grateful that the church was not making any particular demands and felt sure that once more God would show me the way forward.

'Have you achieved what you expected to this year?' I was asked as we moved into the second year of the ministry. It made me stop and review the year. We had been drawn into the life of the church with great affection. New things had started, or were planned, among them a ladies' Bible study which attracted especially our young mums, and the introduction of a monthly family service. Brian and I were enjoying working together but it had not been as easy as we had thought! It was the first time that he had been around at home all day—and calling for cups of coffee while I was engrossed in something else—and the first time he didn't have a secretary to do odd jobs for him! It was the first time we had tried to share a car. Previously we either had two or he had used the train for work. It was the first time our jobs had invaded our private lives and seemed to take us over seven days a week! It was also the first time we had had to work together as a team and I soon learned the necessity of preparing well but being prepared to put aside my plans and ideas. At first I found it hard when my ideas were rejected, especially if I had worked on them feeling God had been directing me. But I came to see that Brian too put things aside and that God had put us together to direct and guide each other. We had to learn not to give and take but to give and receive from each other.

The children too found themselves 'shushed' away from Dad's study, obliged to answer the telephone with the necessary courtesy and to keep the television down! That wasn't too bad in school time but in the holidays it was more of a problem. Another thing they had to accept was the fact that there were phone calls and conversations which they would not be told about and that some of their questions would not be answered. We were grateful for those times when their misdemeanours or problems had remained confidential family matters, for we were able to explain that others too wanted certain things kept private.

I also remember the time when our first 'gentleman of the road' arrived. I sat him in the kitchen and made him a cup of tea and a sandwich. My daughter eyed him suspiciously while she continued to make some biscuits and when she heard her younger brother arrive, she rushed out to warn him. A few moments later a pair of eyes peered enquiringly round the fridge just to see what a real life 'tramp' looked like!

It was a similar gentleman who first showed up our naivety. I was at a friend's house, Brian at home, when there was a knock on our door. A man stood there asking if the vicar would marry his daughter. Once in the study he seemed to have a coughing fit, sending my husband scurrying into the kitchen for a glass of water. When the man recovered and the conversation could be resumed, Brian became aware that all was not what it seemed. The man then requested to pray in the church and left. Feeling suspicious, Brian went into the church and found an empty purse—my purse. I had been foolish enough to leave it lying around in Brian's study!

He phoned me to check how much had been in it. There had been no money but my credit cards were missing. 'I'm going to find him,' he said. I was very concerned about this so my friend's husband drove me back home. We passed our car parked by the side of the lake which is in the centre of the village. Stopping, we could see Brian remonstrating with a man, now standing knee deep in water, swishing around in the water with his hands—much to the consternation of the poor fisherman nearby. He had been peacefully fishing when two men had come running down the path. One of them had then waded into the water right by him. Questioning the man proved unsuccessful—he maintained he was simply 'digging for worms', and eventually we reluctantly gave up, as the fisherman had already done. We rushed home to check that he wasn't a decoy! With wellington boots, my husband returned to the scene. The man had now departed, and Brian was able to dig up my credit cards from the reeds in the lake.

What fools we felt; but it proved an amusing incident to recount later. It became even funnier when last year the same chap had the cheek to knock again and ask for some money! Brian said, 'I know you. Do you remember what happened last time you came?'

'Yes,' he replied, 'I took your wife's purse. Sorry guv . . . could you let me have some money? I'm starving.' He didn't get money but we gave him food—which we insisted he ate outside!

Our first year was not quite what I had expected but I certainly learned a lot. I think I had hoped to be more involved in the community, but the work within the church seemed to have taken all our time. I had made very few contacts outside of it which I really regretted. The children were now old enough to take themselves to school, so there were no school gate contacts, and the evenings could not be booked up because Brian would more than likely be out, so no evening classes were possible.

It was during the second year as I reviewed my lot that I had phases when I felt depressed, when I didn't seem to be achieving anything. It seemed as if I were reacting solely to the needs of others, and had no opportunities to initiate new things, or to control my days. These phases weren't continuous because on the whole I enjoy being with people and there are times of great encouragement when problems are solved as God works in people's lives. However, I eventually reached a point when this feeling of lack of achievement didn't pass and instead I felt a growing resentment against those around me. It seemed as if I was everybody's slave, my husband's unpaid secretary, the cleaner who had to chase around tidying up after everyone, the person who was for ever picking up the pieces but with no recognition, no reward and very little thanks. It seemed to me at the time that the problem lay in the fact that I had no official position in the church; I had no authority, could not act on my own behalf or suggest any initiatives. I have always been an enthusiast who likes to get into things, set things in motion and make things happen and I felt squashed, as if I were drowning. I concluded that I must have misheard God. He couldn't have called me to work in the church like this. I would better use my gifts if I returned to teaching. At least there I would have a position, be recognised, be paid, be in control and feel I was achieving something worthwhile.

The impossible and unbearable alternative seemed to me, at that time, to be that God was calling me to work as Brian's unpaid secretary, to act at his bidding and spend my time as the servant of others. Of course the voices kept resounding in my head, 'The Master was the servant of all. You can ask no more than to follow in his footsteps. He had no position, no recognition, no pay. He was not angry and resentful.' These voices only helped to deepen my sense of failure and lack of self-worth. I was a terrible Christian. God probably didn't want to use me anyway.

One of the worst things about having problems as a minister's wife (as it can be for a minister), is that you have no 'minister' to turn to. Of course my husband did his best, but I'd always land up getting mad at him! He didn't seem to understand fully and I didn't want to burden him with my problems when he was busy with everyone else's. Despite that, one afternoon Brian put his pen on his desk, swung round on his chair and said, 'Right, we are going out for a walk. We must talk this through. It can't go on like this!' So we drove out to the nearest park and walked.

'I really don't think I am being proud. I just need to know that what I am and what I am doing is worthwhile,' I found myself saying. 'When you were called by God that calling was recognised by others and you were ordained into the Baptist ministry. I felt that same calling but it wasn't right for me to be ordained too. I knew my calling was to be different but no one recognises my call. Maybe they do appreciate what I do but they think I do it because I am your wife. I'm just your shadow, an attachment to you and I don't feel that I have any space to be me—or develop my own gifts.'

On returning home, we sat in the study and prayed together. It was hard for me to risk asking God the question I had voiced to Brian but I knew I must. The previous day I had been flicking through Isaiah, preparing a Bible study for our ladies' group. I read various passages. None had been particularly significant but as I prayed the voice of God seemed to bring back to mind one verse. I started saying the beginning of the verse before I realised how it ended. 'I have called you by name . . . you are mine—thank you, Lord—when you pass through the waters they will not overwhelm you. . . .'

God knew how I was feeling! He had called me by name, as an individual, but he was also calling me to face those waters that threatened to drown me, knowing he would protect me. I wept, but I stopped struggling and then the waters did not seem so deep or so turbulent but they felt warm and calm. I didn't know what that meant for me in the future but God had confirmed his call to me and I must follow and trust him.

For me, that was a turning point. The situation did not change dramatically but I did. And having faced it with me, so did Brian. He made much more effort not to interrupt my work by his demands; this I had explained made me feel that he considered his work more important than mine; and as a result I more readily put aside my plans if I could, when he needed last minute help. We gained greater respect for what the other was doing.

Up to this point I had been working with the children and young people. This was expanding and we decided that someone was needed to co-ordinate the work. Having stopped struggling, it seemed as if God was opening up an area of responsibility for me and that he was now calling me to head up this area of the church's work. The youth work team was small and had suffered from many changes of personnel but our 5–7 year old group was expanding and we had just started an 11–13 year old youth group which had grown overnight to about forty. I was pleased with the challenge.

Of course the pastoral visiting, counselling, sermon editing and theological debating continued. I was still involved with the ladies' Bible study and we were thinking about starting a mothers' and toddlers' group. I was being asked to speak at various ladies' meetings and I was still trying to find time to be with my teenage children who I knew needed to talk when they wanted and not at my convenience! So having established a call and found a challenge, I realised that I needed to stop and work out some priorities.

My husband and family, I felt, should come first which

meant that although I didn't want housework to be a high priority it had to be done for the comfort of us all. I seemed the best qualified to organise this, even if I didn't do it myself. This in fact means that most weeks I do it. My daughter is becoming increasingly helpful and I am still working on the males! The family priority means that I also try to be flexible during the holidays and after school hours so that if I feel I am needed by them I can be available.

The second priority seemed to be my calling to the youth work. I spent time developing the work. We set up evening clubs for each age group and linked ourselves with Crusaders.

The last area was the rest of the church work. I had to limit the work I was doing among the ladies, and wasn't able to do so much pastoral visiting. I missed this, but felt that for the time being the youth work was what God wanted me to do. I continued to share with my husband in counselling and with marriage preparation classes but as we only have two or three weddings a year this is not too time consuming.

It is a real privilege to share so closely in people's lives and be involved in their weddings but it can have its snags! In our church we have an arch over the place where the bride and groom stand. This looks very good covered in flowers but it has taken us a while to work out a system of attaching them. An hour before one wedding I went in to check all was well and found all the flowers had fallen off. Dressed in my wedding outfit, I had to climb a ladder, armed with blue tack, and hope my flower arranging skills were up to it. All through the wedding I prayed that the flowers would not fall on the bride's head.

There are joyful occasions to share with people and also the sad times and the problems. The amount of time spent counselling and praying with people varies from week to week. Some situations are ongoing, others as the result of a crisis which has arisen. Had I not become involved in the youth area, I was considering doing some marriage guidance training with RELATE. Maybe I will consider it again in the future.

Among all these priorities I also made sure that we had time off. Brian and I learned early on how important it was to relax and spend time together. We have one day off a week when we normally go out and have lunch or a picnic in the summer. On the occasions when this day has been squeezed out, we have soon noticed our bodies and our tempers suffering—not to mention our relationship. Practically it is important and spiritually too. Brian was preaching about the Sabbath and the importance of a day of rest one Sunday morning. He asked the men in the congregation if their wives had a day of rest, especially those with young children. You should have seen their faces!

I felt better after having set out my priorities and much more able to say 'no' to things I couldn't do. It eased the guilt of feeling I was letting people down, and I was able to enjoy better the tasks I was doing.

One of the things I had always regretted was my lack of contacts outside the church. As our own youth work settled into a routine I realised how few young folk we had contact with considering how many there were in the schools. The pull towards schools came again but not to go back and teach. This time I wanted to be able to go into schools and take assemblies and start Christian Unions. As I thought and prayed about it I realised that it would be difficult to go in with a denominational label so I decided to contact Scripture Union and see what they said.

As I explained my vision to the schools worker over the telephone, he said, 'Praise the Lord! I have been praying for more co-workers. The area I cover is far too large for me.' We met and we talked, and he encouraged me to make contact with our local schools. Two booked me to take primary school assemblies straight away, one school said they would contact me, and one was at that time less enthusiastic.

We had had a joint churches children's crusade a few months before my first visit to the schools. I went in with my guitar and the words of a song and struck up, 'God's not dead . . . he is alive!' All 200 children took up the song—

many having learned it at the crusade. The headmistress had never seen them sing with such enthusiasm! 'God's not dead—he is alive!' I felt it ringing in my ears as I left.

The schools work has grown over the last year. I take assemblies regularly once a month in the primary schools, and in the high school we run a Christian Union each week with about forty youngsters attending. We meet for half an hour, usually start with a quiz or a game and then have some Bible teaching. From this has come a small nurture group which meets after school once a week.

Last year we held two school missions in conjunction with Scripture Union. The first was in February at the high school when a team came and took assemblies, religious studies lessons and lunchtime clubs. We had 200 plus each lunchtime which was very encouraging. The first assembly went very well but with more 'props' than had been planned! One of the team members acting the part of someone who was clumsy and stupid managed to accidentally knock the school flowers flying, adding reality to his acting, but causing him great concern! Fortunately the vase stayed intact and we are sure the assembly will have a lasting impact!

We also had a mission in the primary schools when the Scripture Union Youth Volunteer and my daughter joined me. We took assemblies in four separate schools, clubs at lunchtime and a few lessons. We also took three junior church clubs during the week, in the evenings.

Scripture Union provided us with a parachute which proved great fun and made a good visual aid for the lessons and clubs. We based the assemblies round the message 'God sees us on the inside', and for our visual aid we injected ink into fruit which we then cut open. It is an effective visual aid, but comes with a hazard warning: 'Don't sit in the line of fire while this is being prepared. Faulty needles have a habit of spraying their contents everywhere!' My kitchen and my daughter had a nasty touch of measles—the black variety—and our Scripture Union volunteer had a very red face! I laughed heartily until I realised that I was covered too! Fortunately soap powder and elbow grease overcame the problem. It is fun working in the schools, building relationships with both children and teachers.

'What does your wife see as her role?' we had been asked when we first arrived. It has been a struggle working it out and no doubt in a few years' time the priorities will have changed, but it has evolved and is still evolving. No two weeks are the same and I can never complain about being bored. Tired maybe, angry maybe, but never bored. Working with people and for people has its ups and downs.

I sometimes feel hurt and let down when the youngsters don't turn up—especially after I have worked hard to prepare something—but there is nothing more rewarding than to see God break into people's lives and to watch as their lives slowly change. It is worth all the struggling and the trying to be patient!

So my life is a mixture of support for my husband's ministry, my own work with the young people and my expanding work in the schools. This week, as well as writing this, I have been designing a brochure for the promotion of the church's building project—gathering everyone's thoughts and ideas together, working out the Christian Union programme for next half-term, making several pastoral visits, and preparing for my part in the monthly family service, which I will take as usual with my husband and another church member. Another week I will be taking assemblies, the weekly high school CU, practising and singing with the music group in order to help lead the worship, or preparing and leading the 'God Spot' in our youth club for young teens.

I have no official title, no official job, just the one I feel that God has called me to do. I have made my priority those things I believe God has called me into and that others, including my husband, have confirmed are right for now. I get stuck when asked to fill in forms which ask for my occupation. If I put 'housewife', the house would be justified in complaining that it didn't get enough care and attention if it were my main role in life! Yet if I put minister's wife, schools worker, pastoral counsellor or youth worker, none would quite define the role! And the name and address of my employer? Well . . . !

3

Complementary Ministries

by

Di Williams

Di Williams is a non-stipendiary Anglican deacon at King Charles the Martyr Church, Potters Bar, where her husband Ray is the vicar

I often wonder how it is, as the only daughter of such cautious, unadventurous and conventional parents, I should have come to live life on such a large and varied canvas. Our family style began ordinarily enough. But, married now for thirty years, Ray and I have survived the joys and traumas of what has developed into a unique and in some ways extraordinary family experience. During this time we have acquired seven children, two of whom are adopted, and two grandchildren with another expected. Also, part of our vicarage context is a large assortment of animals, together with many people who have lived in our home for varying lengths of time, to become an enriching and valued extension of the family. And now, to cap it all, I find myself an ordained woman in the Church of England!

Why?

I had always been a good, well-behaved child, seeking to do my best to please the adults (parents and authority figures) in my life. There was never really anyone to be wicked with anyway. And, although unconscious of it at the time, I was lonely. Teenage years passed smoothly and bleakly and from this period I emerged as an adult, rebellious, insecure, needing to be needed and also to prove my competence, and an ability to manage more than anyone else. However, these negative aspects have been taken by God and are being slowly transformed. Rebellion now usually takes the form of independent and careful thought about issues. Needing to be needed is becoming in me a sense of being deeply loved—by God, my family and my friends. And I no longer need to be omnicompetent, but just competent enough!

'Di, will you shut up and listen to me?' What strange and unlikely words apparently put into my mind by God towards the end of a visit I made to South Africa late in 1985. I didn't understand, though I soon would. I needed to listen to God very carefully indeed over the coming months. 1985 had been a momentous year in our family life. Rosemary and Louise were married in June and August. Roger became twenty-one and Ray and I celebrated our silver wedding. November had found me in Grahamstown, South Africa, visiting the Sisters of the Community of the Resurrection. Knowing that I had reached a watershed, leaving behind the period of being first and foremost a mum, I would now be able to look to the future. Suddenly there was space, but I had no great desire to fill it. I was busy, and contented enough, still with some family around, a vicar's wife, and welcoming an endless stream of guests into our home. I was also happily and heavily involved in the life of the church.

Two days after my return home from South Africa God spoke again but this occasion was very different. It was at a lunch for clergy and wives that a seed was sown, or rather was germinated; a seed which grew with alarming speed. The occasion proved typical, for me that is. As so often, I found myself trapped, plate in hand, at a loss for conversation with a stranger. Casting around for topics, I finally discovered that this gentleman had a wife who was training to be a deaconess. Not daring to leave this subject lest I were unable to find another, I pursued the conversation down every available alley: Why? What? When? How? As we left that lunch I knew God had spoken again. I said to Ray that I wondered whether I should think about deaconess training and his reply was encouraging.

From that day onwards, every time I opened the Scriptures my mind began to turn the words into sermons communicated to a sea of faces before me. Yet this was ridiculous, for never had I envisaged myself in such a role! But now God intensified the pressure. I remembered a comment made in the church years earlier when I had been asked when I would be 'preaching in this place'. Another time someone else ventured, 'I knew you would,' as I tentatively shared my thoughts. 'You would be restricting the growth of others into leadership if you refuse to move on,' said two more people.

The call crystallised still further as I attended a Christian Listeners tutors' workshop early the following year. It happened in three ways within a day or two. First I spoke to a deaconess who proved very warm in her encouragement. Then at a healing service which was a part of the workshop, as I went forward to receive ministry, I found myself asking for prayer as I sought God's direction for the future. I was anointed with oil, and I was amazed at the significance that it came to hold for me. To this day I can remember, not only the event itself, but the imprint of the cross in oil on my forehead which becomes a great source of confirmation and strength, especially as I face new or particularly difficult tasks. And thirdly, as I read from Isaiah 49 at the communion service, my heart was pounding as I sensed the words were relevant to *me*: 'Before I was born the Lord appointed me,' and later (v6): 'I have a greater task for you.' All these interwoven strands seemed to me to constitute a call which now had to be tested.

The following months saw my diary littered with appointments as I negotiated the usual diocesan hurdles, sometimes alone, sometimes with Ray. Leaving Oak Hill after my interview, with an acceptance as a potential student, the most significant words to remain with me had been spoken by the student who showed me the college. 'If they accept you they won't fail you,' he had assured me. I don't really know if that's true, but it certainly kept me going through many a subsequent sticky patch!

Then in September of the same year, the final hurdle of an ACCM selection conference eclipsed all else for a few days. The day after the conference had ended I received news of the bishop's phone call as I pushed my trolley round Sainsburys! I was to begin training the following evening! The speed of events left me breathless and not a little amused as the family appeared with gifts—a furry pencil case from one, a 'frog' pencil sharpener from another and an awful lot of teasing about 'Mum's homework'.

The shock of the next few weeks defies description. In Potters Bar I 'belonged', at home and in the church. I was an 'important' person, key to the well-being and happiness of others and in that environment I felt secure. At college I was lost, physically, emotionally and spiritually. I sensed that I was exposed and very, very unsafe. The training decided upon had been one year as a full-time student and a further year on a part-time basis. My fears, voiced to the chairman of the selection conference amid tears, seemed at this point to be well-founded indeed. 'Di, when you cease to be scared you'll no longer be doing a worthwhile job,' he had said. By the time the college term was three weeks old, I could find my way around, had made some friends and negotiated that dreaded obstacle—the first essay.

But then there was a major crisis. Ray, on his birthday of all days, had a fairly severe coronary. What now? Should I give up or press on? It was a difficult decision. In retrospect, I have no doubt that the choice to keep going was the right one. And I was happily unaware of the opinion of those who felt I should abandon training to care for Ray. He wanted me to continue, I wanted to continue and I believe God wanted me to continue too. I hope that the rightness of that decision is now obvious in the ministry which we share together.

It was a struggle, and also a challenge, as I divided my time between hospital, home and college. I found the staff and students at Oak Hill a quite unexpected source of loving and prayerful support, even though I'd only recently met them. As I write I am reminded of my tutor who said that I would remember Oak Hill for its people long after I had forgotten what I learned there! Often I slept during lectures, sometimes not turning up at all. Writing essays began as a nightmare and finally became a challenge I was to face very adequately. However, because of my own reticence and because of Ray's illness, I never completely felt a part of the college community and I would have benefited much more had I been able to contribute more effectively.

This was the first time, too, that I had been thrust into a predominantly male environment, and for an only child with an 'all girls' school background, this was somewhat alarming. Discovering that men too were human, I could never really understand women who were aggressively feminist in their approach, as some were. At college I was always treated with respect and as an equal, for which I am thankful.

Because of Ray's illness, my training was inevitably both more brief and more sketchy than it would otherwise have been, and I emerged from college in some respects ill-equipped. In my reference, my college tutor wrote, 'How Di has trained only God knows, and I mean that seriously!' My ordination after one year was awe-inspiring, thrilling and also surprising since 1987 had seen the approval of the ordination of women deacons passed in synod. I find that I can conduct a baptism with enthusiasm, a wedding with joy and a funeral with compassion, while leading worship and preaching are both a challenge and a privilege. If my academic training for ministry has been deficient, the rich and varied experiences of life afforded by the family have more than made up for it.

There is a powerful innate urge in me to create and to nurture. That's obvious within the family context, but extends much further to the varied animal life around us— dogs and cats, sheep and goats, ducks and hens. They are an integral part of our life and ministry as they live in and around our home, peacefully and productively bringing a sense of harmony and quietness. This creative urge, which I see very much as being bound up with being a woman, reaches further than the home—to creating groups, creating a worship environment, creating a quiet day for a parish and in co-operating with God's Holy Spirit to create new life in individuals.

The 'open door' style of our family living means that we live our private lives rather publicly. Little is hidden of either joy or pain. We have all found it hard, though some, naturally, more so than others; but we have discovered on the whole that with all our imperfections, and sometimes outright disasters, we feel greatly loved and supported. At the same time, people seem more able to trust us with their own pain and failure. Sometimes the children have rebelled, and rightly so, over unreasonable expectations laid on them, by us or by others.

Family sagas have been and continue to be innumerable, like the day one was expelled from Climbers for roaring like a lion from inside a box when his name was called! At times, Dad has been implored, 'Don't embarrass me by wearing your dog collar when you take me to school.' As children, all of them disliked church. Yet now, as adults, five of them have a deeper and more mature faith than I had at twice their age. Our struggles and griefs have been an encouragement to others in a way that our 'success' would not have been. I am convinced that all children are hurt in some ways by their parents, for none of us is perfect. I am equally convinced that as God brings healing and wholeness to my life so he will to theirs as past traumas and failures are opened up to him in order that they may become a rich foundation of new life for the future.

Our adopted, mixed race son and daughter still strive more or less painfully towards adulthood, seeking their roots and searching for purpose. Often I feel fearful and anxious for them, and yet I am grateful. They are a gift. As a parent I yearn for a rich and fulfilling relationship between us. One day I was musing over my longing for them and it seemed my greatest joy would be if they came into the house saying, 'Hi, Mum. How are *you*?' In that moment I understood something quite new about how God longs for me to relate to him, and it has in some sense become the kernel of my own prayer pattern. I also identify with that same grief in the heart of

God over his own adopted people who care so little for him.

Our married life, like all other marriages, has had its ups and downs. The worst 'down' began when Ray was selected ('a late developer' he says) for training for ordained ministry, and it lasted until he was settled in his new sphere of work. A full-time demanding career, part-time training and seven children (two of them only babies) very nearly sank the boat. Contrary to other people's assumptions I was not the ideal and fulfilled mother, and I felt tied, trapped and very jealous as he went to his training, leaving me with the family. My understanding of the pressure on him was minimal. I was angry with him and with God. However, the boat gradually began to float once more and we survived—with lots of counselling, lots of prayer and lots of loving friends.

The best of our marriage is now, or maybe even to come. We have grown a lot, understand one another better and are more tolerant and appreciative of our differences. We work together as vicar and deacon, thankfully within a richly gifted and varied staff team so that we are not, I hope, seen by the parish in a somewhat confusing 'dual' role. In personality we complement one another, though in some aspects of our work we clash. We usually find that we work better 'in parallel' than actually together.

Ray would have made a good salesman, which is in fact what he is, as he constantly seeks to reach new areas where he can chat about the gospel. It matters little whether this is with the swimmers with whom he exercises, with the dog walkers in the fields before breakfast, or while sick visiting at the hospital and going round factories on the local industrial estate. He returns from such excursions rejuvenated. He's a great enthusiast and this is contagious—unless, of course, one disagrees with his point of view. He quite enjoys a battle, though his heart does not! Necessary time spent at his desk he finds frustrating and he looks upon it as a waste of time. He likes to be out constantly among people. He is the one who attracts people to the church.

By contrast, I am not good at any of these things. My forte

is in caring and nurturing. A wife and mother, I find one of my richest areas of ministry has been among young families where I am able to relate in a way and with an ease that perhaps a man would not. The strands linking baptisms, a mums' and toddlers' group and our fairly new adventure of informal morning worship are strong, and this has become a real growth area for our church. My need to seek solitude for prayer and for preparation is great and I spend a day a week away from the parish for this purpose. I enjoy time spent at my desk and I don't function well with a timetable crowded with people. I find it fulfilling to prepare sermons, retreats and quiet days and to spend time with individuals, talking and praying at depth. Ministry works well for us as long as we stay broadly within the confines of 'he gets them and I grow them', though of course this isn't always possible. If Ray is irritable, he's usually had too much time in the study and if I'm irritable, it's because I've had too much time with too many people. However, Monday is our day off and people and the study don't feature, though a pub lunch, shopping and animals usually do! We find it increasingly necessary to spend time together and to put a ban on talking 'shop'—very difficult since we enjoy our work so much.

How others in the parish experience my ministry is coloured by the fact that I started out ten years ago as a wife and mum, and so I was known as Di long before I had the role of deacon. So I'm sort of home-grown, and the tremendous sense of rejoicing over my ordination experience seemed to reflect their joy, my joy and God's joy all rolled into one. I have felt my ministry since then to have been both welcome and challenging. I must say though that the acceptability of my 'up front' role in our church had been very much prepared for me by others. The last ten years have seen much change so that there is now a mixed choir and a lady organist. One of our readers and a server are women who had gained the respect of the congregation long before they moved into their present roles.

Funerals have been the focus of much of my ministry beyond the church family. In the early days our local undertakers always made a point of asking a family if they would mind having a 'lady vicar'. Just a few did. These were usually very 'fringe' church people who felt only the vicar (male) was 'proper'! As time has gone on the undertakers do not now ask the question and the problem has disappeared. Ray and I are both at ease taking funerals and it usually happens these days that a family asks for whichever one of us they already know.

Because we are married to each other people often think that our ideas are interchangeable. When we disagree in public therefore, like in a PCC meeting, they find it embarrassing, not knowing who to support. If on the other hand we agree, they think we had it all 'sewn up' over the morning tea—which just occasionally is true! So you can't win!

In no sense do we see ourselves primarily in ministry to support each other, although of course we do this, but not in any stereotyped vicar/curate role, where I fill the gaps and do those things traditionally expected of a curate. Some of these things Ray does and others are carried out by other members of the staff team. Rather, we work in complementary and independent areas, fulfilling the ministry which God gives us according to our very different gifts and inclinations.

Working with colleagues in the team has always been a joy, for it is here that we meet monthly to plan worship and share out the workload. And not only this; we seek to understand one another as we eat, pray and talk together. I see this as a real safeguard against what could otherwise have been seen as a 'gruesome twosome', excluding others from participating fully in responsibility and leadership. This group consists of the vicar, deacon, two readers, one reader in training, an ordinand on placement and another lay person experienced in leading worship—seven in all.

I have a firm belief that output equals input, constantly finding that if the former exceeds the latter for too long I run into difficulties. I jealously guard my places of input, and I delight in and am grateful for each of them. Of course this has to be different for each person, but these are mine:

1   Two patches of quiet a day—about one-and-half hours altogether.
2   A quiet day each week, to talk, pray and prepare. For this I go to the Sisters of the Community of the Resurrection of which I am an Oblate (a lay member of the Community living in the 'world' and following a simple way of life).
3   About two training workshops/retreats a year.
4   Day off with Ray (I do spend other time with him too!).
5   Time with two or three special friends.
6   Time to read—spiritual books not directly related to current output, and some 'light' reading.
7   Animals—a great resource, relaxing, enjoyable, peaceful and never in a hurry. As the goats eat the layers' pellets, the hens eat the goat mix and the dogs eat the duck food, everyone is suited, and life is after all happy and hilarious not only for the animals but for me too!

As I have been writing this chapter I have been increasingly aware of the unique nature of God's call and of his work in any individual life. The value of working as a team where each person is able to contribute his or her own gifts has been highlighted for me. At times I find ministry to be utterly exhausting and sometimes frustrating, but at the same time I am content, fulfilled and very happy. I am grateful to have had this opportunity to share my experience.

4

Called out of Failure

by

Rose Barrett

Rose Barrett is minister of Edmonton United Reformed Church, and Free Church chaplain to the North Middlesex Hospital

My call to the ministry came originally when I was a member of a Baptist church in Westcliff-on-Sea, Essex and halfway through my nursing training. The call initially was very clear—it was to preach! My church was very evangelical with about 250 members and still growing. There were more than fifty of us young people in our teens and twenties. Our minister tried to encourage me (or perhaps get rid of me!) by involvement with a youth team of three or four others and we honed in on struggling village churches in Essex.

My application to the ministry through the Baptist Union wasn't too well regarded by the Essex Baptist Association—they preferred 'bright young men' to go to Spurgeon's College in South London. I certainly wasn't one of those (I wore a mini-skirt in the 1960s!) and neither was I academically brilliant.

The suggested solution was for me to go to the Bristol Baptist College and take a three-year training course with a few other women students there, for what was still the Baptists' Deaconess Order. I wasn't too happy with this suggestion—the deaconesses still wore hats—and I felt called to the ordained ministry, but it was a start even for me to go to college at all. So I entered Bristol Baptist College in October 1968 at the age of twenty-one.

Three years later I came out, much wiser in some respects

but very shaken up in others. Fundamentally I was very unhappy in myself: I had struggled to cope with an environment which challenged me in every aspect; intellectually, socially and spiritually. The emotional insecurities I had as a young woman, about being an adopted child, from a working-class and non-Christian family, with few expectations on achievement, with a gnawing hunger for love and affection that was never easily satisfied; all of this inner turmoil had led to several disastrous and promiscuous love affairs, a mild reactive depression and a 'wilderness experience' of the mind and spirit which lasted some further three to four years. I had failed the London University Diploma of Theology exams which meant that my plans to go on to a place for youth leadership training at Westhill College, Birmingham, were quashed. I was unemployed, unqualified and returning to my home in Essex as a failure.

Eventually I found some work, first as a barmaid, then as a residential helper at 'Greenwoods', West Ham Baptist Mission's Christian therapeutic community in the village of Stock near Chelmsford. Here I stayed for one year, gaining more than ever I realised at the time from the centre's patiently loving and perceptive resident minister, the Revd Ronald Messenger. Following 'Greenwoods' came a brief entanglement with the Civil Service at VAT headquarters in Southend.

But also during this time God led me into contact and then church membership with the newly formed United Reformed Church. I came into the URC through the love and openness of Christ Church URC at Rayleigh, Essex, and also the graciousness and acceptance of the Moderator of the Eastern Province (as it was then). With the encouragement of this new church I was able to pick up the pieces of my life, to help with a junior church group on Sundays, and on weekdays with the junior section of the Boys Brigade Company, and then in time to resume lay preaching in the Southend-on-Sea district of the URC. Very slowly God was trying to cut away many of the thorns preventing the blooms emerging from this very prickly 'Rose'!

In 1974 I gained a traineeship in social work with Hertfordshire County Council. This meant a move to Letchworth for one year and continuing involvement with the URC there; then on to study for my professional diploma in Applied Social Studies and the CQSW at North London Polytechnic in Highbury. I lived at Crouch End and became an associate member at Union Church, a joint URC/Baptist congregation, where I discovered that my social work tutor was the church secretary. I continued lay preaching with the Central London district of the URC and was invited to serve on the church and society panel. After completing my training I had to return to Hertfordshire Social Services Department and fulfil a two-year contract. I became a social worker at the Psychiatric Department of Queen Elizabeth II Hospital, Welwyn Garden City, and joined nearby Hertford URC. My lay preaching ministry was now within the then Enfield-Hertford district.

Then came another turn of the tide. Around 1978–79 at Thames North Province's annual weekend conference, held at High Leigh, the main speaker was the Revd Bob Gordon. A conversation with him and a request on my part to receive prayer and ministry for inner healing led me gently into the experience of baptism of the Holy Spirit; and through this I gradually came into association and increasing involvement with GEAR (Group for Evangelism And Renewal in the URC), and the wider charismatic renewal movement. This was the decisive moment of handing over control of my life (and all its inner tumult and conflicts) to God. It was the beginning of my learning to keep more in step with God on a daily basis, consciously choosing and seeking to follow the way of discipleship with Jesus—my Lord.

It was after some eight years of running away from the truth about myself, and then facing up to who I was and getting into the place where God wanted me to be spiritually, that the original call to Christian ministry was reaffirmed by him. The opportunity was reopened, I candidated with the URC and to my surprise (because I expected with my history to be turned down) they agreed with my call. After some haggling about academic and theological requirements at my assessment conference, I had the wonderful gift of spending a year's training (a theological 'refresher course') at Westminster College Cambridge.

I was ordained in July 1980. My first 'joint' pastorate at Tooting in London SW17 was demanding and difficult. I inherited two churches: a former Presbyterian, St Peter's, and a former Congregational church at Mitcham Road. The two separate sites were a mile away from each other, but in quite contrasting neighbourhoods. My time there involved presiding over the closure of the former St Peter's, the faithful core of members going to nearby Balham URC, while those who had commuted in from a wider distance were encouraged to attend churches in their home neighbourhoods. St Peter's site was sold to the New Testament Assembly, a growing Black Pentecostal Fellowship, whose tithing of money, time and talents achieved in five months what the Presbyterians hadn't managed in the previous fifty years! There was a transformation of decline and decay into new life. It was a faith lesson not lost on me.

I then faced the need to be prophetic with the remaining church near Tooting Broadway. This church couldn't face the reality of inner-city ministry—with decaying buildings, declining membership and dwindling resources. They didn't want to let go of the memories of former glories. And letting go, dying to self, meant relinquishing hopelessly unsuitable buildings. My style of ministry wasn't readily appreciated! My presentation of the gospel and the beckoning direction of the Holy Spirit was too threatening, so after three-and-a-half years I had to move on. But, praise God, some three years ago another minister came, and Brian Ranford's gracious and gentle ministry has helped the members to face reality, to release resources and to see the site redeveloped to provide sheltered housing and a multi-purpose worship centre.

So I moved on, across the River Thames to North London and an associate ministry at the growing and exciting Palmers Green URC. It was a very happy experience for three years to be a part of a theologically diverse, loving and serving Christian community, under the direction of its gifted minister, Revd Keith Forecast. After three years at Palmers Green, I moved two miles across the A10 road to Edmonton, a smallish pastorate of some forty-five to fifty members in an urban, multi-racial and multi-faith part of the London Borough of Enfield. In our URC parlance it is a 'two-thirds-scope pastorate' which means that one-third of my time is to be used as the Free Church chaplain at North Middlesex Hospital. This is an expanding District General Hospital—with all departments and with teaching hospital status too. I serve as one of the team of four chaplains: an Anglican priest, a Roman Catholic priest, a Roman Catholic religious sister and myself covering all the Free Churches.

Thus I was called . . . from weakness and failure, into realising my vulnerability and my total dependence on the overwhelming and restoring grace of God. I try to serve him, because I know he is the real 'love of my life'—but I often think I do not serve him very well.

I am a single minister, and while opportunities do present themselves to this child-free and mortgage-free state that would not otherwise be possible, I do sometimes feel, quite cynically perhaps, that the main opportunity it gives you is to work yourself into the ground. Some churches will willingly let you do that; that is, unless you set your own limits on what you can give and contribute, and what you can and cannot do, in order to protect your own interests and allow time and privacy for yourself. I don't feel, for instance, that some of my congregation are particularly good at being aware of my needs. They don't, on the whole, seem to have the capacity to empathise with me and the tiredness I often feel, both physically and emotionally. When you are single you have to affirm yourself and your abilities quite a lot. If you are conscientious and something of a perfectionist for the Lord's work, you will probably brood over your failures and tend towards introspection as I do (usually late at night!). My biggest weakness probably is that I don't suffer fools gladly! I express my frustrations at the conservatism I see in the church, and its lack of response at most times, by verbalising it: a 'short fuse on anger' is how one of my elders describes it! But usually, once my anger and frustration are ventilated, they are gone and not harboured.

Overall I enjoy the challenge of being at Edmonton and I am aware of the immense privilege and responsibility involved in being a minister of the gospel. But the lonely times are usually when I am tired, when I have had a difficult and tense elders' meeting, when I know I have failed people or God in a pastoral capacity, or when I've fallen behind on my work schedule. It is during those times when you feel so stretched, and there's no one around in the middle of the night to cuddle up to, to give you a hug, to tell you simply, 'You're okay!' that you have several choices: do you pray harder, read a book or watch a video, or ration out the whisky? Well, I'll leave people to figure out which of these options (if not all four) I'll normally choose!

But the wonder of the Christian ministry is that there is always another day to be faced, and in the Lord's gracious and tender mercy to us, he forgives our failures, he can redeem our mistakes, he can empower and equip us with his Spirit and he makes each day new.

Money and the ministry is something that cannot be totally ignored, and yet it is a tricky subject to mention. I think that money (or the lack of it) for ministers' stipends, and the local church's attitude towards its clergy can become an emotional battleground. The United Reformed Church has a scheme to give every stipendiary minister in the church the same level of basic stipend, irrespective of whether they are female or male, single or married, with or without dependants. Fundamentally it appears a good system as it tries to be fair. It saves us nowadays from the old congregational system of each local church deciding and then paying the minister their own local stipend. It means that the resources for ministry are seen as a commitment of the whole church throughout the United Kingdom. Also, if one's local church treasurer is not very efficient or supportive, you are spared the embarrassment of having to ask, 'What has happened to this month's pay cheque?'

However, there are anomalies in the system. For example, those pastorates that can afford to are allowed, even encouraged, to pay a supplement to the minister, as an addition to the basic stipend. 'Supplementary earnings', for example for chaplaincy, teaching, or using any specialised skills outside the church, may be retained by ministers, if this doesn't come under their pastoral scoping (and so counted as part of their stipend anyway). Housing is usually provided by the local church—most ministers are not in the position of being able to afford their own homes, so they live in the church's manse. These come in all shapes, sizes, states and conditions of repair or disrepair. They could be modernised, bodged or non mod-con!

But emotionally you feel caught in a peculiar tension: if like me you are a single minister, your income is likely to remain the same and have to stretch the same for the foreseeable future. With house prices as they are, to own your own house seems an impossibility. Yet to live in the manse can also create tension. You are grateful to have the security and privilege of a (free) roof over your head, but you know you don't own the house, yet you have to make it home. Also it often has to serve as a base for pastoral interviews, office administration, hospitality and a place for larger group meetings. All of the repairs and maintenance contracts for any work on the property have to be agreed with the congregation's lay leaders—whether that means dealing with a fabric committee, a board of management trustees, or elders. You don't have 'carte blanche' to knock down an ugly and awkward wall, or cover an overgrown, weed-laden garden with concrete paving.

To give one instance of the kind of battle to be faced, it took me eighteen months to convince the elders of my present church that we had to demolish the wall and small patch of front 'garden' in order to provide a drive-in forecourt for the car. There is no garage with this terraced house, and the verbal fights with other residents in the small cul-de-sac over parking access were causing me physical problems. Although the church realises that I am effectively 'on-call' six days out of each week in the year, it was a struggle to get them to realise the need for legal parking access.

Other fights have been over double glazing, faulty window frames, provision of a working-surface in the small, restricted kitchen, and retiling the old and depressing bathroom. Every time the first option has always been to go for the cheapest thing possible. The discussions about cost and workmanship take an average of six to nine months to bat around elders' meetings, back to the congregation's church meeting and remitted to the elders again before agreement. It is tedious and profoundly poor stewardship. But also, it is emotionally draining to feel, as a single and now middle-aged professional woman, that each time I want something done I have to fight my corner against a group of cautious, conservative and unimaginative older men. Often the feeling implied from the result of these encounters is: 'She's only a single woman without a family, so she can put up with anything.' But if you haven't got a convenient man to hide behind—as your husband, boyfriend or sympathetic friend—then being firm in standing by what you feel is needed (because you do have to live there!) doesn't exactly make you popular.

Guilt is always near the surface too, because I know that there are vast differences between the lifestyles and incomes of various church members. There are those who are in the professional middle-class income bracket who have pleasant and comfortable homes to live in, while others in my church are on lower incomes, pensions and welfare benefits. For example, one older lady has lived in a privately rented property and coped most of her life without an indoor toilet or bathroom and no instant hot running water. Therefore if I seem to be demanding better standards for the manse am I being selfish and putting an extra financial burden on the church? Or am I being realistic—knowing the comfortable standards enjoyed by the more affluent church members?

Another source of frustration is the lack of perception and support in fulfilling my material needs: as a Christian I try to honour God by tithing my stipend and I try to aim for the gross rather than the net amount. I give half the tithe to two Christian agencies each month and the other half to my local church by deed of covenant. In addition, I have several other covenants for smaller annual payments distributed throughout the year. My standard of living is probably relatively worry-free—no mortgage (for reasons given earlier), no children and no pets. I manage, I hope, to live fairly modestly, free of debts, no bank overdraft or credit card accounts. I also have regular monthly commitments to meet in addition to the tithes; for example, insurance policies, monthly television rental, small building society savings, television licence, food bills, wages for my weekly cleaner and domestic help (who is a necessity, not a luxury!) and also a car loan repayment to the church. But I am now taxed with other URC ministers by the Inland Revenue on the 'benefits in kind' received by living rent free. I am aware that within the limits of my stipend I find it very difficult to save up for any major household item or foreign holiday. There is not a lot to spare from my regular expenses on each month's stipend.

A comment by a church elder got to me recently and it shouldn't have done. We were discussing a recent pastoral exchange undertaken with an American minister and his family and myself. One of the elders said, 'You haven't got a dining-room suite, nor a washing machine or tumble drier in the manse and the Americans are probably used to all these mod-cons at home.'

I agreed. 'That's true,' I said, 'but there is nothing I can do to provide these, given limited space in the manse and a limited income to buy them.'

'Oh well,' said another elder, 'they will just have to go to the launderette with their washing like everybody else.' And he laughed.

Unfortunately it was the laugh that did it. I am afraid I bit my tongue and said nothing further, and I have regretted it ever since. I wanted to say to him, 'Well you jolly well don't have to go to the launderette because your wife does your washing in your machine in your home every week.'

A few weeks later I overheard the same person in an ecumenical discussion group say that at this stage in his professional life he and his wife have more money now than they need or know what to do with. Well I could have made a suggestion: let me have the cash to get a washing machine and tumble drier to use in the manse! In fact it is my local vicar's wife who does my laundry every week because she knows I can't afford to buy a machine and yet she also feels that I shouldn't have to spend hours out of my one day off in the week sitting in the local launderette. She acts towards me out of the sheer open-hearted goodness and kindness that many people love about her while my elder closes his eyes and ears to my particular domestic situation.

Now this may appear to be unduly and heavily labouring a point, but often in the ministry it is the more trivial issues that cause the frustration in the local pastorate; those pinpricks that somehow burrow beneath the skin and find their target to irritate, to create resentment, bitterness and frustration. My experience on the whole is that it is these immediate issues that cause trouble, and major doctrinal arguments and disagreements rarely come into it. It is the tensions in personal relationships, perceptions and pressures that cause the problems to loom large and at times appear overwhelming if one is under stress, feeling undervalued, overworked and unappreciated. How the devil can have a field day in the Christian community through these issues! How at times I would like to be free of the 'private chaplain' expectations crowding in from the local congregation, and seek some refuge and relief among 'happy pagans'. I think I understand why the Lord Jesus occasionally enjoyed, even preferred, the company and jokes and camaraderie of the 'tax-gatherers, publicans, prostitutes and sinners' he was at times invited to wine and dine with. They were in total contrast to the uptight, sanctimonious criticism of the

Pharisees' 'table-top conversation' and their at times ungracious hospitality!

If we're not on our spiritual guard, the experience of the 'colour of money' in the Christian ministry is likely to be dyed green with envy at what we don't have and pink with jealousy and red with rage at the lack of generosity and narrow-minded meanness that are at times exhibited by members of the Christian community. And yet, we realise we are serving a Master who tells us to 'seek first his kingdom and his righteousness' above all else; who himself had no material possessions, nowhere to lay his head; and yet he, the Son of God, who in heaven was 'rich beyond all splendour' for the world's sake and my sake, gave up all that he had and became poor, humiliated, dishonoured, disowned and dispossessed. Because the colour of money—on the cross—is first black with my sin, and then red with the precious shedding of the Saviour's blood, his ransom payment for me. And that is where the balance of my heart, my wallet and my values has to be found—at the cross.

'Do you do weddings?' A colleague and friend of mine, Sheila, and I often share this phrase as a private joke. It seems remarkable to us that often when people who are quite outside the church discover we are ministers their automatic question is: 'Do you do weddings?' They rarely ask, 'Can you celebrate Holy Communion, do baptisms, conduct funerals, or lead Sunday services?' The question uppermost in their minds is about 'doing weddings'. I've puzzled over this. Is it somehow deemed to be indecent for a woman to officiate at the celebration of two people pledging their lives to each other in marriage? Is it the question of who will appear at the church wearing white, the bride or the woman minister?

But such a question leads me to look at a fundamental experience for women in ministry: coping with ignorance. Part of the ignorance is displayed by those who are 'pagans', that is they never bother with God or the church at all, until they are forced to acknowledge the church's existence at the sharpest points of pastoral need: a funeral, or, more often for the URC, a request to remarry a divorced person. The other level of ignorance lies regrettably, I must say, with lay people in the other churches of this country. Here, I'm afraid, I will be less polite about the Anglicans and Roman Catholics! For the lack of awareness about the sixty to seventy years' history of the valuable contribution to Christian ministry made by the ordained women in the Free Churches, commencing with the Congregational Churches in the early 1920s, often makes me very irritated and not a little angry at the way we are marginalised. It is difficult enough to hold your corner among the abysmal ignorance of the secular world (for example in industry, the media, among health professionals and teachers), but among those who should be our fellow pilgrims together in the British churches, well there is no excuse!

I had occasion, albeit reluctantly, to correct an Anglican churchwarden at an exchange of ministers service during the Week of Prayer for Christian Unity. He introduced me as, 'Miss Rose Barrett, the deaconess from the United Reformed Church.' I corrected him immediately, 'No, it's the Revd Rose Barrett, Minister of the United Reformed Church.' ('And don't you forget it!' I muttered under my breath.)

Now saying this makes me sound arrogant. I realise that the Lord Jesus had strong words to say to his disciples about their jockeying for position in the kingdom of God, and I don't want to invite his displeasure, but there is a point at issue here. To try to put it simply (and I realise that I am about to enter into the usual well-trodden minefield of theological arguments) I want to say that as far as I am concerned about the work I do and the person I am, my particular part of the 'One Holy Catholic and Apostolic Church' (on earth) has recognised my calling to be a servant of the Lord Jesus Christ, employed full-time as a minister of the word and sacraments (with exercising pastoral care of a local congregation). We must never forget that it is the Lord Jesus who calls women and men to discipleship, to follow and serve him. It is the Lord who, through the gifting of his

Holy Spirit, equips every woman and man to serve him in his church in the world. I seek to serve my Lord and Saviour to the best of my ability, in a particular role which the United Reformed Church has affirmed in testing my vocation, and which the church has seen fit over the years to describe as the ordained ministry; a ministry which is organised and structured in a way that has many similarities with the ministries of our male colleagues who are priests, deacons and ministers in the other historic churches. But I am aware of those churches' histories and structures. I try to be an informed, 'spiritually literate' Christian! It is the people who are uninformed and 'spiritually illiterate' members who are the problem, and who, in the Church of England especially, would like to brush aside the Free Churches' women as being of no significance to them, when they could see us as a model for ministry to their divided church.

My experiences of Church of England chauvinism come most strongly when I am invited to attend the institution of a new vicar. It is on these occasions that you see and feel the old boy religious network really working! The churchwarden comes into the room where we are robing for the service; 'Good evening, gentlemen,' is the opening gambit! Then the processional line up commences, and the women deacons and Free Church ministers usually fall in as the 'tail end charlies'. Here my paranoia gets to me and I start to shake at the thought of tripping up, not dividing at the right moment to my allocated choir stall but following the bishop to the altar or pulpit by mistake!

I once had an enlightening lunchtime discussion with a Roman Catholic priest who was uptight about me wearing a clerical collar. 'Why do you have to wear one?' he said. 'It is not a very feminine garment!' In a way he's right—but I looked at the issue with him in this way: 'I have a right to wear a "dog collar",' I said, 'because my church has affirmed my calling. It's an easy mark of identification for people around to know what and who I am, in the same way that police officers, fire fighters, nurses, doctors and barristers have their uniforms. If I wear an ordinary dress and a cross people will think I am an Anglican deaconess or layworker, and I'm not. If I wear a special kind of dress, people will think I am a Roman Catholic nun, and I am certainly not that! So what is left to show that I am an ordained minister? It may not be feminine enough for your liking, but that's your problem, not mine!' And that was the crux of it for him—the image of femininity versus masculinity.

I tend to back off from those church women's meetings that want me to come and talk about 'being a woman minister'. I maintain there is no such thing. I am a minister of the gospel—it just so happens that I am female rather than male (a biological accident?). I know the old joke about there being three sexes in the world: men, women and ministers. If it is easier, then yes, I feel that I'm in the third gender category! There is both a female-ness and male-ness in me as a person, but I've not analysed the proportions of this.

I stand or fall in my ministry on the level of the quality of my relationships with other people. It's to do with my personality, not my gender. Some people will appreciate me as Rose, others will and do not. I know I get up the noses of some people rather than others, but often these feelings are subjective and intuitive, more to do with the guts than the head. Some members in my congregation describe my style of rather directive leadership as being 'Thatcherite'. I don't know whether that is meant as a compliment or an insult, but as I'm no supporter of the Tory party I guess it must be an insult! And you see, the people using this tag are for the most part older men and women in their sixties and seventies, who describe strong women as being 'aggressive'. They don't use the description of 'Thatcherite' when talking of my male friends in the ministry; they have 'leadership quality'!

I do not play the role of the 'helpless woman' or the 'little girl' figure. I am who I am. I will always try to be open, forthright and honest, and I expect that of others. I am who I am, again, through my early experience and emotional fights to survive and discover my true identity as the beloved daughter of my sovereign heavenly Father. That has made me tough!

I am passionate about the gospel too. It is life for me! It is the core, the *raison d'etre*, of my existence! As Simon Peter said in John's Gospel, 'Lord, to whom would we go? You have the words that give eternal life!' If I left Jesus now, where would I be? To whom would I go?

But I am concerned about the Christian church too (in its widest sense), because for twenty to thirty years it has been my family. And so I am concerned about the church locally, in its mission, to be involved in sharing the gospel in all ways it can, to save souls, to bring women and men and children to the Lord, to save them from judgement and condemnation, and to lead them to receive God's great gift of salvation. I do find it difficult then to curb the enthusiasm in my heart, and to settle for a quiet, comfortable, complacent Christianity, which most of our congregations seem to opt for, because it is safe.

To be passionate about the gospel! That is the hardest tension of all, as the minister of a small and struggling congregation that finds change uncomfortable. Bishop Festo Kivengere spoke some years ago to clergy at Southwark Cathedral. He said that the worst 'crime' of any Christian or minister in this country (he meant Britain) is to be enthusiastic about Jesus Christ and on fire for the gospel. In other people's eyes that makes you too radical! I have found that to be so true unfortunately, since my first steps in renewal from 1979 onwards. I long to see my congregation changed, renewed and revived with the fire and power of the Holy Spirit. I long to see us starting to add a holy, God-inspired imagination and breadth of vision to our ministry as a small church in a multi-cultural urban neighbourhood.

A recent three-month visit to the United States last summer has taught me much about being open to new things; about taking initiative and risk, in a sense to market the gospel. I am aware that people do have a deep hunger for God, yet so often we ignore that. The people in the two pubs next door to my church do have questions, thoughts and feelings they want to explore and have answered. They want to believe in something or someone, they tell me. And they feel that my faith is somehow a missing 'magic' ingredient that they don't qualify for; they cannot get hold of it for themselves. I find that a tragedy. And it is an even bigger tragedy to see the great gulf between my congregation and the pubs' regulars; somehow no one is bridging it. The 'sinners' in the pub who enjoy their drinks are very afraid of crossing the 'invisible line' of conformity and religiosity to come in through the church's doors. The 'sinners' in the church, who enjoy their hymns, are very afraid of crossing the pubs' thresholds, where the 'demon drink' is sold and enjoyed, to share the gospel. Who can bridge that gap? Only Jesus can! I try to be the bridge with him by being there for both groups of sinners—at the church and in the pub.

'Lord, set us on fire with your Spirit, to renew both the church and the publicans. Set me on fire Lord, as your servant. Don't let me be afraid of my position, or of the leaders of my church who may disapprove of my methods and message, and seek to remove me. Let me be single-minded and whole-hearted, Lord, for you and the gospel!'

I often feel that the experience of being a minister (female or male) is that you are, humanly speaking, always in a 'no-win' situation. You cannot please every member of your church all of the time. You cannot please the faithless, irreligious pagan world all of the time. You have to be faithful to God though rather than worry about being successful in your ministry. Faithfulness is required when the work is hard; when people misunderstand you, try to thwart you, ignore and reject you. You have to be faithful in receiving both praise and criticism—to honour the Lord who has called you. My model for ministry has been, perhaps surprisingly, the prophet Jeremiah.

He was a young man when the Lord called him to his prophetic ministry and he felt totally inadequate for the task. But the Lord promised to be with him. Jeremiah often found himself in difficult and dangerous situations. Yet he showed a level of perseverance, steadfastness and courage that has rarely been equalled. He was abused, attacked, beaten, chained up and imprisoned. He was thrown into a well and left there to die, either by sinking into the deep mud and drowning, or succumbing to the starvation caused by a long siege of his city, Jerusalem.

Jeremiah was threatened with death on several occasions and there were moments when he was overwhelmed by misery and felt abandoned. Yet the Lord stood with him, rescued him and delivered him wonderfully from Israel's enemies. And throughout, Jeremiah was faithful to proclaim the word of the Lord, even though at times he experienced great anguish of spirit.

I think that's the quality of ministry I am called to try to obey and fulfil. How I need to depend utterly on the Lord to fulfil his holy will in my life!

5

Motherhood and Ministry

by

Rosemary Harrison

Rosemary Harrison is a non-stipendiary Anglican deacon in the Kinson team ministry, Bournemouth, where her husband Richard is a team vicar

Only decades ago, a woman's role was considered to be firmly home-based. Her daily chores were limited to menial household tasks and to caring for her large family. Today, society has moved away from this image, and many women struggle to combine the pressures of being wife and mother with part-time or often full-time employment outside the home. Frequently, the need to return to work is financial, particularly in our more materialistic society. But, apart from that, many women, better educated than ever before, need to find stimulation and job satisfaction outside their homes. Whatever the reason they must be highly organised, so that they have time for employment, time for their children, time for their husbands and, if there is any time left at all, time for their own interests.

In a regular nine-to-five type employment, this is difficult enough, but the situation I presently find myself in can so easily become a source of conflict and tension, as I grapple with the demands of being wife, mother and deacon. I am the wife of a vicar, living and working in a busy inner-city parish. It would be easy enough to allow that to become a full-time occupation. Certainly the traditional vicar's wife could spend every hour of every day answering the telephone, listening to cries of help, making endless cups of coffee, rushing round visiting sick, lonely, distressed or angry people.

If that were my only role, life would be greatly eased! However, combined with those expectations and pressures are those of being mother to two little boys, aged eight months and two years. Outside the home I am also a non-stipendiary deacon in the same team ministry as my husband. It is a situation that I probably would never have chosen for myself, but one which I believe God has gradually, but very definitely, led me into.

My call to ministry came first. As a reluctant, sometimes resentful, vicar's daughter, anything to do with full-time Christian ministry was not a consideration. I was well aware of the strains and stresses of vicarage life and I understood the loneliness of those who were in full-time ministry. In times of family or spiritual crisis, who were they to turn to? I had grown up conscious of the spiritual platform on which we as 'the vicarage family' were elevated. Clergy families were not supposed to have any real problems, and if they did, they would always come out smiling and full of God's peace and joy!

So, when I had to embark on some kind of career training, anything remotely connected with church work was avoided. Although my own faith then seemed quite strong, it had not yet stood the fires of testing. I was secure in the faith of my parents, and had seen and experienced God's faithfulness to them and our family. But my own faith had not yet developed enough to be detached from that of my family. God had much to teach me. . . .

Like so many of the Old Testament leaders—Jeremiah, Moses, Gideon—I did not consider myself a natural leader. My school reports often described me as 'shy, quiet, lacking in confidence', but, gradually over many years, God used day-to-day situations to increase my trust and confidence in him. Each time I asked, 'Why me, Lord?' he gave me the strength and ability to carry out the work which I believed he had called me to. Each new challenge was another step nearer to being able eventually to stand up as an ordained leader in the church—although at the time I was blissfully unaware of that future work!

Becoming head girl of the senior school I attended was perhaps the first step towards the position of leadership God had planned for me. It was, I remember, a position I greatly feared and yet God daily gave me strength to continue. But I was still not prepared for the change of direction in my career plans. Instead of the social work training I had envisaged, I found myself embarking on a teacher training course. The work itself was not difficult, but being a student in a distinctively non-Christian, even anti-Christian, environment was my first real taste of the outside world from which I had been sheltered all my life. Here I experienced ridicule and mockery because of my faith, but with the support of many praying Christian friends, I and my faith survived. I had never really longed for teaching as a career. I certainly loved children, and had actually spent four months after leaving school working in a residential children's home. But I could not imagine ever being confident enough to stand before a class of thirty or more children, to teach them. There were times during my training and even first years of teaching when I felt like giving up. But, during three years of training and seven years of teaching, with friends and fellow teachers continuing to encourage me, God developed in me those qualities I would need for the future work he had planned for me.

After ten years of teaching, I found myself again at a crossroads. In my own local church, I was committed to some activity almost every night of the week—from children's work and music, to Parochial Church Council and its various sub-committees. One Sunday, I joked with the vicar about taking up permanent residence in the church. 'Perhaps you should be a deaconess,' he said. Those words seemed suddenly to carry a hint of reality. For some time now, I had questioned my heavy involvement in the church, combined with the advance preparation and planning needed for teaching. The two occupations were beginning to conflict. My commitment to church activities seemed to be dominating my desire to teach enthusiastically and thoroughly. So, once again, I began to seek God's will for my future.

The vicar's 'joke' began to develop in my mind. Could God want me in full-time ministry? I realised and remembered again the hardships and disadvantages of this kind of work, especially if I were to enter it alone, as a single woman. I tried to dismiss the idea, but God obviously had firmly planted it in my mind, and there seemed no escape from it. At a parish weekend in Chorleywood, the vicar there made a passing reference to me one day becoming his deaconess. Was this another joke or was it a serious suggestion? He intimated that I should prayerfully consider the suggestion, to discover the reality of this call.

Soon after that I attended a weekend conference to explore and learn about the realities of ministry. I listened, with some apprehension, to the stories of both men and women in full- or part-time Anglican ministries. They were honest and realistic, sometimes painting gloomy as well as encouraging pictures of their own experiences. I knew that I would have to make some considerable sacrifices, and must expect some loneliness too, if this was the kind of work I was to pursue.

For at least three years I would receive no regular income, and when I did, it would be considerably less than my present salary. In the school where I taught, I was a woman among a majority of women, with only three men on the staff of eight. In the Anglican ministry, my position would be reversed—I would be a woman in a man's world, where many still did not realise the value of a woman's ministry. Finally, but perhaps the greatest sacrifice for me, I would have to sever the strong links with my home church; it was the church I had attended since I was a toddler, where my father had ministered for over twenty years. Although he was no longer the vicar, I was still heavily committed to the church family there, and my faith was very much home-grown. Despite the three years I had lived away from the security of this evangelical stronghold, my faith was still narrow and too comfortable.

Such a background was definitely a disadvantage and almost a hindrance as I approached the director of ordinands and later ACCM. My faith was thoroughly examined and scrutinised by the director of ordinands, who suggested that I apply to a non-evangelical theological college in preference to one of the more evangelical. However, I eventually selected one of the latter, which was rapidly growing and open to all traditions and denominations of the church.

As I pursued this call to ministry, it was as if I were walking down a long corridor similar to those in hospitals, with a series of swing doors to push open. Each step towards ministry was like another door to push—the doors of the director of ordinands, her consulting panel, the bishop and finally the large, heavy door of ACCM. Even as I faced that final door, I was still not convinced that this was the direction God was leading me in. However, the doors leading to it had all opened. Even the county education officer was prepared to accept my late resignation when I knew the results of the ACCM selection conference, which was held in the school vacation.

I believed that the eventual outcome of this conference would be God's direct purpose for me. Eventually those doors did swing open, revealing to me the way ahead—to train as a full-time accredited layworker.

The prospect of living in a Christian environment and having time to spend learning more about my faith was attractive, but not realistic. Although I already realised the need for my faith to be challenged, I was still unprepared for the pain of such an experience.

Suddenly, I felt devalued among a large body of men and women, many of them more mature and stable in their faith than I was. After seven years of being the figure of authority in the classroom, I was once again the student who had to listen to and obey those in authority. Instead of the homely little cottage with its own garden where I had lived previously, home was now confined to one tiny study-bedroom, and a shared kitchen, bathroom and lounge.

At the age of twenty-nine years, such a change in lifestyle was quite a shock, and I felt almost void of my own identity. It took some months to adjust to this new role. Many times I longed for the comforts and familiar surroundings of home, and particularly my home church and family. In addition to grieving for my home church, I began to undergo a great loss of my original, home-grown faith. With parents and parent church far away, the time had come to grow my own individual faith and dependence on God. Before that could begin, the original plant had to be uprooted and replanted again in ground where it could eventually grow bigger and stronger.

The uprooting and replanting was a most painful experience. I began to learn and even experience some of the questions and doubts concerning faith written about by many other theologians. Never before, or since, have I experienced feeling so far away from God. Yet, never before had I experienced daily worship so rich and varied. Those times seemed to bring me closer to God again and often reassured me of his presence, despite my doubts and fears.

Discovering more about the Christian faith was not the bed of roses I had often dreamed about. To continue the analogy, there were plenty of unwanted branches to be pruned before a fine bed of roses could bloom.

I had not foreseen this aspect of my training for ministry. I knew of the academic and the practical training, but had not realised the full implications of the testing of my faith. It was however a necessity in order to equip me to minister later to those who themselves had little or no faith, or who were experiencing a crisis of faith.

I commend the college staff who were usually available to support and encourage in these times of turbulence. In particular, I valued and respected the advice given by our very patient, wise and godly tutor of women. This quietly authoritative lady commanded the respect of even the most long-standing members of the faculty. She never appeared bitter, angry or resentful towards those who could not accept the place of women's ministry. And yet, she was neither weak, nor unable to express clearly her commitment to the ordination of women. Her example of tolerance, together with her ability to express a woman's point of view, is one which many of us would do well to follow. I am convinced that every theological college should have such a person on its staff. It should, if possible, be a woman who is also ordained, has experienced some of the traumas and challenges of faith, including the loneliness of being a single woman in a male-dominated environment.

During my college training, the academic course was undergoing constant review and change, as the college was soon to offer its own degree course. Realising the need for women to be as well-qualified as possible, because of their present status in the Church of England, our college principal—now the Archbishop designate—encouraged me to follow this course. Consequently, there was a greater emphasis on the academic training rather than the pastoral.

During the summer vacation, there was a five-week placement, actually living and working in a chosen parish. I chose to work in an inner-city area of Liverpool. There, I worked and trained alongside a deaconess. This short period was the most fulfilling and encouraging part of my training. As I lived and worked among real people again, my call to ministry was renewed. I was able to begin to develop the gifts in me which had lain fallow at college, and slowly my confidence as a leader grew.

While my theological college strongly encouraged female students, it was still male-dominated, and consequently much of the training seemed male-orientated. Most of the students and faculty members were not actively opposed to the ordination of women, but few were actually in touch with or sympathetic to a woman's needs and her different approach to ministry and to theology itself. Many rectors and vicars feel the same—while they are not actively opposed to a woman's ministry, they are either uncertain or have little or no understanding of how to use her fully. A woman's ministry should certainly not be limited to speaking at or leading the ladies' group, the women's fellowship or the Mothers' Union meetings! The training of an ordinand should, therefore, include some lectures and seminars on the possible tensions and conflicts which might occur between a woman and her fellow ministers, as well as her parishioners.

Throughout my time as an accredited layworker, and later as deacon, I have found it important first to concentrate on building up a mutual trust with fellow male clergy as well as parishioners. Male clergy often seem to feel threatened by a woman's ministry. And, if the woman fails to handle the situation very sensitively and carefully, it can easily develop into some kind of competition—male versus female. Many women today still have to walk on a tightrope in ministry. If one small mistake is made, their ministry may be severely impaired or even shattered.

Women in ministry should *not* have to seek to prove themselves. But, as God originally made female to complement or work alongside the male, so I believe male and female should work alongside each other in ministry. The ideal complete ministry consists of both male and female within its team. The family model created by God, with male and female at the centre, should be followed by the church, which is the body of Christ—the Christian family. There should, therefore, be both male and female authority figures working as partners together in ministry. Just as a family without a mother or father figure is incomplete, so too is a church without one or the other. It may function well, but it will not be quite as efficient or complete. So, both men and women need to learn to understand, trust and respect each other's individual ministries. College training should allow opportunities for this to develop.

Certainly for me this was made possible as during my time at college I met and developed a deep trust, confidence and love in another ordinand—the man whom I eventually married. Although he had little or no experience of women in ministry, he respected and encouraged the gifts that women had. He had no feelings of inferiority or of being threatened by the opposite sex. Many times when I was feeling discouraged or disillusioned, he encouraged me to continue and to persevere.

Through those times of learning to trust, our friendship developed into a deeper love for each other and within a year of our first meeting we announced our engagement. We now had to reconsider our respective ministries. Were we to look for a joint ministry in the same parish or separate ministries in different parishes? At the time of our engagement, Richard had already accepted a curacy in Plymouth, Devon. As we hoped to have a family in the near future we decided that if I became a non-stipendiary minister in the same parish, it would be easier to cease working, or at least limit my ministry when our first child was born. The vicar of Richard's first parish was enthusiastic about women's ministry, and recognised my place on the staff team.

Six months after our engagement, we were married, and three months later, with exams safely behind us, our joint ministry began. It seemed an ideal situation, and yet we soon discovered that working on the same job, in the same parish, could so easily produce conflict and tension. For two individuals, who had lived single lives until their early thirties, to be joined together not only in marriage but also in ministry could produce sparks which sometimes led to little explosions! Over the years we learned to respect and understand our different ministry styles and we gradually began to work together as a partnership, complementing each other's gifts.

We discovered too that living and working together in the place of our employment could produce an intense and overpowering atmosphere in the home. Conversations at mealtimes and even on days off became almost entirely church dominated. We recognised the need for an outlet. So I found part-time employment, teaching at our local junior school. Not only did this give me an outside interest, but being at a local school gave me added insight and contacts in the life of the parish where we worked.

Some of our contemporaries at college, who were also led into joint ministry, found it necessary to plan a strict time-table for the non-stipendiary partner. I felt this would be too regimented and would restrict the areas of ministry I was to be involved in. So, together with the vicar, we worked out specific areas of responsibility rather than specific times when I would minister—sometimes individually and sometimes jointly with my husband. Jointly, we led a youth group and a house group, established a monthly worship centre at the local school, planned and led services together and began to develop a limited counselling ministry. My individual responsibilities included participation in the weekly worship life of the church, midweek ladies' meetings, pastoral visits, musical involvement in worship and, later, ministry to young mothers.

In two senses we were pioneers together in this first parish. Richard was the first curate there and I was the first woman minister. I felt it important then to set a positive precedent for women's ministry here. The vicar and his wife both accepted and affirmed my role. I particularly valued the wise counsel and support of the vicar's wife, who although not herself ordained was very active in the church and able to share the feminine way of thinking with me. We valued our weekly lunches with the vicar and his wife. On these occasions we either affirmed each other or ironed out any potential areas of disagreement and conflict between us.

Most of the church family accepted my ministry, but there were a few, who although not actively opposed, were apprehensive and unsure of my role. My natural approach is neither assertive nor militant, so I was able to allay the fears of some who thought I might be an ardent feminist. During this first curacy I never knew of any obvious hostility, and certainly when the time came to decrease my ministry because of the arrival of our first child, I realised how much my ministry had been appreciated.

As well as support from within the parish, I also valued monthly visits to a retired deaconess, still active in her ministry in a neighbouring parish. Together, we shared our concerns, hurts and anxieties, as well as our joys and encouragements. From her wealth of experience, she guided and advised me, still in the infancy of my ministry.

Opposition to women at deanery and diocesan level was far greater. At deanery chapters, I did not feel accepted as a fellow minister, but rather as Richard's wife. Our own vicar, aware of some of these feelings, particularly requested me to lead the service where he was to be made rural dean. However, doubts and opposition still continued. One parish deliberately did not invite any curates to the induction of its new vicar, because they did not wish the three lady deacons in the deanery to attend! At diocesan level, the attitude was similar, perhaps more hostile. My husband was very amused, yet also angry, when he received a petition to sign, asking him to state his opposition to women's ministry. His reply was that he not only supported lady deacons, he was also married to one.

Two years after our arrival in the parish, the first ordinations of women as deacons took place. After interviews with ACCM and the diocesan bishop, it was agreed that I should be ordained. At about the same time as this I discovered that I was expecting our first child. It seemed somehow ironical that, at eight weeks pregnant, I was standing before the bishop to be ordained. He was delighted with the news, but I have wondered how some of the other ordinands might have reacted had they discovered. I well remember struggling to fight back early morning sickness as I stood shivering in the chapel of the rather ancient convent used for the retreat. I survived on glasses of lemonade and plain biscuits before each day began.

Eight months after my ordination, a new role began—that of mother to our baby boy. Consequently there was little time for my ordination to cause any reaction, either in the parish or in the deanery, although a coachload of our church family attended the service at the cathedral, indicating their support.

However, it was not so easy for others within the diocese.

My own spiritual director, in no way a militant feminist, experienced such antagonism from her vicar following her ordination that she was forced to leave both home and parish. However, a neighbouring parish was delighted to have her join its team, and now use her fully.

Now that I had a third role, as a mother, I again had to work out the balance of my commitment. Although I was recently ordained, the bishop, our vicar, my husband and I all believed that being a deacon should take third place. My chief responsibility would be as a mother, and to devote the majority of my time to our family, at least for the next few years. So as my preaching and other commitments decreased, I was able to spend time with the baby I had longed for for so many years. Despite the ever increasing pressure for women to return to work as quickly as possible, we both believe that I should not devalue our children by putting work before them. We are also aware of the development of their own spiritual lives, and are therefore careful that my church commitments are not seen to take me away from them. I am particularly conscious of this, being the product of a vicarage family myself. My father was an extremely hard-working, conscientious priest and pastor, but inevitably time spent with the family was limited to mealtimes and the odd hour during the day. He rarely spent a whole day with us. I remember too the comment of a teenage boy whose father had recently been led to full-time ministry. The churchwarden of the parish expressed his delight at this, but the boy only replied, 'You might have gained a vicar, but I have lost my father.' Our children's spiritual health is as important as that of our church family, but so often it is neglected. As the children grow older, and eventually reach school age, so I shall be able to increase my duties as a deacon.

However, in practice that decision has proved much more difficult to maintain. Only a few weeks after the birth of our firstborn, I sensed pressure from the parish, who were keen for me to resume ministry. 'Isn't it about time you preached again?' they would say. 'We miss your ministry. I hope it won't be too long before you return.' One lady in particular seemed almost jealous and resentful of the time I now spent with our baby. Others would insist on holding him, so that I could be free to talk to or pray with people. After a long wait for motherhood, I was probably especially possessive of our baby, but I felt angry that I was not able to enjoy being possessive. Just as I shared myself in ministry, so too I was expected to share our baby. Such pressures weighed heavily on me and as a result I now believe that I tried to resume ministry too soon. Instead of our newborn baby having 100% of my time, he probably only had 70% as I rushed around the parish visiting various people, baby in pram.

As the end of our curacy approached, we reconsidered the whole area of my ministry. We felt it important to state our intentions to the new parish. These were that my primary role was to be a mother, secondly to be a supportive wife and, finally, to have a limited ordained ministry. As clergy, we are very conscious of the example of family life we need to give. In a society where the family as an institution is breaking down, it is essential to show the importance we place on family life. Young children need the stability and security of an adult who will always be there when needed. So we have made a rule that, most of the time, I will be that adult. At other times, Richard will take on that role. For example, now that our youngest child is weaned, I will be free to lead an occasional evening service while Richard stays behind with the children. This arrangement works well for both of us as it provides a refreshing change from both our daily routines. The children, too, enjoy having their father at home, especially as he is so often out in the evenings. Although there are plenty of willing volunteers to look after the children, we aim to use babysitters infrequently—certainly no more than twice a week, often not at all.

On arrival in our present parish, where my husband is now team vicar, we defined clearly the boundaries of my commitment to both team rector and parish. The team rector has always respected that opinion and has allowed me the freedom and flexibility I need to maintain a limited ministry. Since the birth of our second son this year, this has become even more limited. Most of the church family, too, have understood and accepted the emphasis we place on my role as mother, and I have not felt compelled to resume ministry too soon. Being in the background of parish life is sometimes quite a lesson in humility. While I thoroughly enjoy and value the time I need to spend with our two boys, I long sometimes to be more involved in certain areas of ministry. The needs of our particular parish are great, and there are many sad and lonely people. I long to be able to minister to them, but at the moment, the needs of a two-year-old and an eight-month-old are greater. This inner frustration does sometimes cause tension and conflict in our home, particularly during our second baby's first few demanding months. I still recall struggling to write a sermon for a Women's World Day of Prayer service, with him cradled in one arm and our toddler crying for attention at my feet! My tears of frustration were plentiful.

If my husband worked a regular nine-to-five day, it would probably be easier to return to a fuller ministry. Then, in the evenings at least, I would have more freedom to attend meetings or prepare sermons. However, combining the work of both mother and deacon does not only involve use of time, it also affects my own emotions, which can in turn affect the children. Ministering to people can be very exhausting and often frustrating. Young children are particularly sensitive to our moods, and my elder son especially seems always to be at his most demanding when I am feeling tired. So I deliberately do not become too involved in much counselling work. A stable, secure start in life is very important for young children.

As well as the tensions caused by the limits a young family place on my ministry, there are also those that being married to a fellow minister bring. Having both a father and brother in ordained ministry inevitably gives me a certain role model to follow. That, coupled with my own training and experience, sometimes leads to negative criticism of the ministry of others, particularly of my husband. We constantly have to learn to be honest with each other, and I particularly to express my valid opinion in a more positive manner.

As the children grow less dependent on me, so I shall be able to increase my ministry again. Already I am able to commit myself to certain areas which will not greatly affect the children. Regular involvement in the mother and toddler group and limited preaching or worship commitments are now possible.

However, as the children become more aware of situations, so too will we have to become more cautious about discussing parish matters in front of them. Not only could work dominate our home, but the children could so easily hear something confidential and repeat it later at some inopportune moment. The need to develop interests other than the church is now becoming more apparent.

The life of a vicar's wife can often be very lonely. The position of our house, high on a hill next to the church, isolates it from the surrounding council houses and flats. In any type of parish, whether rural or inner city, as ours is, it is difficult for the vicar's wife to make close friends who can also be confidants. I find it invaluable to have close friends outside the parish. We have some very faithful Christian friends who live in a neighbouring parish. Since we met them eighteen months ago, our friendship has deepened as we prayerfully support, encourage and trust each other in times of hurt, sickness or anxiety.

Our team ministry is also very supportive. The clergy team, consisting of team rector, curate, vicar, reader and community worker, meet weekly over lunch, with their wives and together we share much laughter, anger, fears, hurts and anxieties. The wives in the team are now planning to meet for further prayer and support of each other. My needs as a clergy wife and mother are well met. I have yet to discover support as a deacon, mainly because I have been too occupied with our family to meet many other lady deacons, or to gauge the reaction of deanery or diocesan clergy towards women's ministry. However, our community worker, herself a church army sister, and myself are able to support and encourage each other regularly.

As we look to the future, we cannot know God's plans. Certainly, as our family mature, I envisage becoming more heavily committed to my work as deacon. But if, for any reason, our children require more of my time, I feel that I must be adaptable and able to decrease commitments once more. I would not therefore consider a full-time ministry until the children had finally become totally independent. Time spent with children in their early years can never be repeated, and it is a major influence on their security, stability and dependence in later years.

When eventually I am able to commit myself to full-time ministry, there may well be the possibility of ordination to the priesthood instead of the diaconate. I am certain that God is calling many women to the priesthood, but, as with my first call to ministry, I would be cautious about entering the priesthood lightly. I do feel the frustrations of not being able to celebrate communion, especially as my husband, trained at the same time as I was, has the authority to do so. I recall too the disappointment and frustration felt when I was unable to administer communion to several elderly ladies whom I regularly visited. Instead, I had to ask Richard to come and consecrate the bread and wine. But these frustrations alone would not be the reason for ordination to the priesthood. As God gently guided me to the diaconate, so I believe he will also clearly direct me to the priesthood, if it is his plan.

Being married to a fellow minister does place some limits on the positions which I can apply for. Either I continue in a non-stipendiary role, or I pastor another church in the same team. Alternatively, I may operate a non-parochial ministry, such as a hospital chaplaincy. God has surprised me by leading me into my present situation. Perhaps there are yet more surprises ahead, leading me into a ministry which now I could never plan or even imagine.

'Now to him who is able to do immeasurably more than all we ask or imagine, according to his power that is at work within us, to him be glory in the church and in Christ Jesus throughout all generations, for ever and ever! Amen.'

6

Pursuing God's Call

by

Jane Hassell

Jane Hassell is minister of Victoria Park Baptist Church, Bow, London

In 1968, at the age of fourteen, at a girls' grammar school in the Mile End Road, Bow, I could never have imagined being the pastor of a Baptist church just five minutes away down the 'back-doubles'. Yet here I am and have been for the last five years.

As I sat in a car outside a church building that resembled a large warehouse, I wondered what sort of church this housed and what the church spoke of to the surrounding neighbourhood. The cars flashed by me. The painter, propped on his ladder, glossed blue the large main doors at the top of the stairs in the middle of a paint-peeled Victorian chapel. He waved at me. Later, after I'd become the pastor there, he called me 'Doll' and I thought if I'd been a man, it would have been 'Guv', or I suppose 'John', in East End style. Even to him it was somehow different referring to a woman minister.

As I watched, thought and prayed, the awareness grew within me that this was the church I would soon be a part of and have the responsibility of leading. My name had been suggested to six or seven churches and I wasn't privy to any inside information, but I just had the inner feeling that this was it.

It was at around the age of fourteen that I began talking with friends and teachers at school about the strange faith they seemed to have in Jesus Christ. It took about a year of talking and looking at the Bible to convince me that Jesus was the One worth following. It was promised that he was the One with the power to change the bad in me and develop the good. I was one of the school's mouthpieces for asking pointed and awkward questions, potentially a troublemaker who saw it as her responsibility to test the ability of the teaching staff. The needlework teacher who took a weekly thirty-minute discussion period, which was a threadbare cover-up for sex education and moralising, once told the class she thought I should 'join the communist party or become a trade union leader or something like that'! I only mention the school days because it seems to me that even here God was calling and preparing me for ministry in his church. Few would have seen any potential for Christian service in a mouthy teenager, up to her eyes in the late 60s' experimentation that various Saturday night parties allowed. God did, however, and so did the Christian teachers. An idealist by nature, I was very aware I was falling short of my own standards, let alone God's, so the Christian gospel made sense to me.

While still at school in the sixth form I heard God tell me during one prayer time that I would be used to teach others from the Bible. I was leading the school CU and still had a reputation for outspokenness, but even so felt that God wanted to train me to speak for him; even then a daunting prospect. From the beginning I did long to communicate what I knew about God in the language of the ordinary person, and especially to reach those who had no contact with living Christianity. This desire has only grown with time. It is looking back that often establishes the genuineness of a particular call. I can see the patterns of God's activity and providential planning. It is surely no chance that I should commute to school in Bow for eight years and end up being a minister in the area. Because of this, my understanding and love for the area, and the people's acceptance of me came more easily.

During my time at college and university, more mature
Christians quietly worked away at encouraging me to
develop as a Christian: giving me opportunities to go on
conferences; encouraging me, challenging me about wrong
attitudes; teaching me many things about prayer and the
Bible. They themselves were freshly influenced by the charismatic movement and so encouraged me to seek deep
experiences of God's Spirit. They were utterly convinced,
and so was I, that human ability was never adequate in
Christian service. The pursuit of personal holiness and
Spirit-enabling power was vital. This aspect of personal and
practical encouragement from other Christians would seem
to have a catalytic effect on those aiming to serve and lead in
the church. Women, at times though, may miss out because
there is often no expectation that they can and will be called
to leadership in the church. This varies between churches to
the point of ridiculous incongruity. Personal and group
expectation do play a large part in promoting Christian
service. Non-conformist churches stress not only the call of
God to function in leadership, but also the recognition of this
call by the local congregation and wider church. These form
two of the most important aspects of any concept of ordination. By rightly insisting on both though, we see that some
churches make it virtually impossible for gifted women to
pursue their calling.

My thoughts at college, university and also during two
years of teaching in a large secondary modern were often of
how to get to know the God of the Bible better, and so share
him with the people I knew who were either apathetic or saw
this as irrelevant. At that time I knew I wanted to teach the
Bible and probably work in a church, but the thought of
being 'a minister' had never even crossed my mind. This is
not surprising because the circles I moved in were adamant
that the Bible ruled out women as ministers. While being
dogmatic about this, my senior Christian friends did,
however, advocate a concept of everyone having a ministry
or area of service. In practice, then, my role models of
leadership were of both women and men, and so I was not

deprived of seeing women function in leadership. I never really understood how women were allowed to function in leadership in the para-church organisations and in the church overseas, but denied this in England. The women I unconsciously modelled myself on though were good leaders.

So I went to theological college to prepare myself generally for ministry; where, or doing exactly what, I didn't know. It's not that unusual for individuals to go to Bible or theological college with a desire for further training while also asking God to make these things clear during the course. I remember being fairly vague at my interviews regarding denominational allegiance and what exactly I thought I'd do eventually, and being told I would have to clarify these things while at college or it would be difficult to function. Our course into ministry and leadership may not always be totally plain sailing, but this tends to make us more aware that it is God who guides us through the obstacles.

I chose the Anglican college in Bristol for my training, despite its reputation for being Reformed. To be honest, at that stage I didn't know what that meant anyway, except I was told they would question my description of myself as a charismatic evangelical. My church and friends sponsored me throughout my three years' training and this was a miracle and testimony in itself that God was the Provider. My only other source of income was the few pounds a week I earned washing-up pots in the college kitchen. My two years at Trinity (followed by a year at London University) were very happy ones. I benefited from the excellent biblical content of the course and also from aspects of Anglican spirituality. Nevertheless, it was at this Anglican college that I firmed-up my convictions that I was a non-conformist in my ecclesiology: I developed convictions about baptism, church government and patterns of ministry. Yet it was also here in an Anglican ministerial college, which at that time represented various nations and denominations, that I remained convinced that all Christians are part of the one church.

Looking back I wish that the curriculum had had more of an integrated approach to training for ministry, but theological colleges are still learning to combine the pastoral training with the academic aspects. I've also come to be a great believer that much training should be done on the job and that colleges should supervise urban mission placements and training in situ.

It was at college that some of my assumptions about women and ministry were shaken. For one thing there were women and men there who believed and even campaigned for women to become Anglican priests. I can remember the two women tutors, Joyce Baldwin and Myrtle Langley, both good academics in their fields, occasionally saying things that amazed me. One stunning statement was made during a lecture. The lecturer said something to the effect that God was not male to the exclusion of female. I was dumbfounded and returned to my room horrified to think that such a 'blasphemy' had been uttered. Nevertheless, it was comments like this that made me begin to search the Scriptures, read books and cross-question people about the nature of God, the role of women and New Testament concepts of ministry and leadership. I would say it took between three and four years to change the views I had been taught for over ten years. Ideas inculcated in our early Christian years, and especially by those we love and respect, are often hard to challenge and change. From my background, if I were to teach in the church, I had to be convinced that Scripture didn't exclude all women from teaching in the church.

Much of this wrestling with Scripture was full of painful emotion because I was also wrestling with the developing sense of call and the longing to fulfil this call to be a teacher in the church. My friends, I now see, had to cope with much. I verbally pounced on them when they uttered what I judged to be banal and unbiblical platitudes, for example about the greater gullibility of women to deception. A great tussle was going on within me. I felt God was calling me to leadership and teaching, and yet I had been taught that this was not permitted and so, by inference, I must muzzle this 'Jezebel desire'.

Then one day, during a staff Bible study while I worked with UCCF, a young man suggested I went and talked with Ellie Krieder, who was an elder in the London Mennonite congregation. My lunch and chat in the peace of Ellie's flat, her careful listening to my story and her advice left me walking down the road with a peace and liberty of spirit that I had not felt for months. She told me I was only one of many women (and men) who were wrestling with their desire to be true to God's voice in their spirits and also to Scripture. She advised me to spare my friends the arguments they were hearing, break the isolation and mix with others who had come to believe that even as evangelical Christians they could believe in women leading and teaching in the church. Her acceptance of me and weighing of what I said had given me the room to begin to break out.

One of the women I arranged to meet up with was an Anglican called June Osborne, now a deacon and minister-ing just round the corner from me. We met in a cafe behind the Old Vic and Christian Arts Centre, and she too encour-aged me to pursue what I believed God was saying. Needless to say, I came to the conclusion that enough work had now been done on Scripture to put the onus for textual proof on those who want to exclude women from leading in the church.

I detail this struggle with Scripture and what I felt God was saying to me because I know others, due to their upbringing, are still struggling. This battle was the major hurdle excluding me from doing what I believed God had called me to do. I also knew it wouldn't be easy to take the risk of losing close relationships with certain people, some of whom were my mentors. Most of the friendships survived, however, and many new ones have developed.

I have struggled on and off with the question of whether marriage precludes certain types of ministry or the reverse.

At one time this seemed a more acute dilemma for women.
Again, with my background and certain 'evangelicalisms', it
was assumed that the woman/wife was by nature and design
the principal or only home-maker and would always fulfil a
support and therefore secondary role of ministry to her
husband. Again I just hadn't thought things through and so
for a long time I carried an unresolved tension: is it either
marriage or ministry for women? Watching married Christians function and fulfil their ministries either jointly or
separately, and share the home-making tasks, including
child raising, is convincing enough proof that for some,
ministry and marriage is their gift. For others, singleness is
their gift, and ministry is fulfilled from this perspective.

A new development in my sphere of experience is to see
marrieds and singles, male and female, fulfil their ministries
together. Their varied giftedness means they complement
one another on the team. The eight deacon leaders in the
church I belong to, as well as their physical and spiritual
giftedness, are male/female, black/white, single/married,
older/younger. Some of those married have spouses who also
have gifts of leadership, and other spouses don't.

There are advantages and disadvantages in being married
and in being single. What would seem to be a vital ingredient
of all our lives, though, is community and the caring commitment and task sharing that comes from this. As well as the
community of the church, many people (though not all) also
have families. There would seem for most of us to be varied
balances needed between time with people and time on our
own. For me this works out well to share a house and
community with another Christian and also various lodgers
at times. I also need some hours on my own most days if I am
to be able to meet the demands of leading worship and
teaching on most Sundays and meeting people all week.
Good friends are vitally important to me. I value their
company and advice and would find Christian leadership
much more difficult without them. For this reason I have a
support group of eleven friends in a variety of occupations
who meet with me three times a year to pray and question

with me. At other times we meet just for meals, chat and fun. It is perhaps a mistake to think we will get all the support we need just from within our family or even our church.

Once certain hurdles had been navigated or indeed removed, I was free in my praying to ask God: 'What now?' I was a member of a large and thriving Baptist church which also had Restoration involvements and I knew women in leadership here was a no-go area. Single women in ministry was also somewhat of a non-thought-out area. During a quiet day of prayer with fasting, where I sought to have my question answered, I felt the word and answer 'ordination' clearly impressed on me. This was strange because it's a little-used word in most Baptist circles and personally I am pretty anti-cleric in my theology. I also didn't even know if women could be ministers in the Baptist denomination. I did not know that many Baptists had recognised women as pastors since 1922. Despite this they are still few and far between. The assistant pastor of my church informed me of this and at the same time told me that he and others thought this was unscriptural. By this time, though, I was strong enough in my assurances of what I believed God was saying not to be swayed. Having previously done three years' theology, including two years' ministerial training, I was loath to return to college, although I realised this might be a requirement. As it turned out, after stringent interviews I went on a residential selection conference. Their recommendation was that I go forward to pastor a church, although I had to do some further study on the job. Church officials were constantly warning me that settlement in a church would be very hard as many congregations would still not call a woman leader. Again, it didn't work out that way. From the day of answering the question—where and how I was to fulfil this ministry I'd been preparing for for so many years—to becoming pastor of a church took five months.

Perhaps it is worth saying that I do recognise that there are dilemmas for many as they consider the leadership of women. Some are not prepared even to look at Scripture in a new way or consider the possibility, but there are others, genuine and willing enough to rethink, who still with a clear conscience wouldn't call women to lead and teach. If there is enough mutual respect and trust, this may not preclude working together because we each recognise that we give account individually and ultimately when we meet God face to face.

The church of which I am the pastor and overseer of a team of lay leaders, invited me to lead and so there has not been dissension about having a woman leader. Sometimes there are a few unfortunate jokes, but predominantly it's been a rich experience of learning and leading. I believe for the moment God hand-picked the area for me and fitted pastor and people together. Most of the church and its various attached friends and family live in the very mixed urban area of Bow. There are both extremes of plush prosperity and powerless poverty, and a larger group in the middle. Situated in what is generally a working environment, the church is a strange concoction of people: a colourful mixed salad as well as a melting pot of cultures, types and nations. At our Harvest Supper a few days ago we munched our way through samples of West Indian, English, Nigerian, Chinese and other sorts of food. We are a developing community of worshippers and witnesses to Jesus. One of my joys has been to begin to see not just numerical growth, but some people beginning to use their gifts in service of others, and with a growing spiritual confidence. It would be a dreadful thing if the one-man-band type of leadership were replaced with a one-woman-show. This nurturing of local leadership takes time and genuine desire for co-operation.

A woman pastor who appeared clearly evangelical was quite a shock to other church leaders in Tower Hamlets. The more liberal leaders seemed pleasantly surprised, the reformed leaders of missions and congregations warned their people off, some of the evangelicals came to put me right and the others kept their heads down. I had to pray hard, breathe deeply before speaking carefully, use my Bible well, refuse to argue, and laugh a lot to ease the tension. The church also received some flak in the form of a few critical letters. I'd love to say this has all totally vanished in five years, but only two months ago one of our members was told that our whole church was damned because there was a woman pastor. Maybe things like this will always happen—I don't know.

Amazing things have happened, however, in that about fourteen churches in Tower Hamlets have formed an association of evangelical churches. We are slowly learning to pray, celebrate and evangelise in the open air together. We have seen the beginnings of a life-skills college for the unemployed in Spitalfields. This greater co-operation is a work of God's Spirit and was brought into focus at the beginning of Mission '89 by a prophetic exhortation: 'Before you go fishing you must mend your nets.' The kingdom of God is likened to a drag-net (Mt 13:47) and there is a real need for individual churches and leaders to stop the isolationism of 'rod and line' mission. The 'broken net' indicated that relationships have needed to be mended and strengthened as we have practically sought to 'keep the spirit of unity in the bond of peace'.

No doubt there are many things to be worked through yet, but those will have to be dealt with with integrity as they arise. Individual ministers in the group seem to have resolved the presence of a woman minister in different ways. To be honest, I receive the encouragement and friendship from those who favour women's ministry and don't probe too deeply about how the others resolve it. There is just too much else to do in the shape of thousands of people in the area who don't know Christ.

I have never received an adverse comment about women in ministry from those I've met outside the church. In fact quite the opposite: people are usually very favourable, understanding that women are generally culturally better prepared to be involved in the caring professions. Some are still disbelieving because their stereotype of a minister is not standing before them. Social work departments, hospitals, schools and the police don't seem surprised at a church leader or representative who is female, even one who may well be wearing jeans, trainers and a sweat shirt. Women's ministry is guaranteed to be a topic of conversation with relatives after a funeral or other major event and can be an easy inroad into sharing the gospel of Jesus.

It's an interesting thought to realise that our view of ministry and leadership says very loudly to the world a lot about our beliefs concerning the nature of God and of humanity. Post-Calvary we live in the genuine New Age; the age of the fulfilment of Joel's prophecy (Acts 2:17–18, etc). The Holy Spirit is to be poured out on all Christian people. Women's ministry is an eschatological sign of the times. There is no elite class of priests, but a priesthood of all believers. There are a variety of gifts, including leadership gifts, which are to be used to enable others to serve with their gifts (Eph 4:8,11–12). The gifts Jesus gives are for all Christian humanity. No distinction is made to preclude women from certain ministries. Leadership is modelled on the Jesus way of servant authority (Phil 2). Moreover, Scripture and practice reinforce that this leadership is stronger if grounded in a team of fellow-workers. The world can see in a mixed team that Christ has broken down every dividing wall and there is no class or racial or sexual distinction which raises anyone above another (Gal 3:26–29).

Those who adopt a solely male pattern of leadership are perpetuating the error of the God who is male to the exclusion of female. It reinforces a belief in a male God who doesn't transcend sexuality and is most truly represented by the male of the species as many have suggested. What we are saying about the nature and spiritual capabilities of redeemed women if we exclude them from leadership is highly disturbing. Scripture clearly says that both male and female are in God's image. The New Testament makes plain that Jesus' treatment and respect for women was totally different from the Jewish and Roman world into which he was born.

Day by day as I live and work in East London, I am trying to share Jesus Christ with those around about me and to encourage and enable others to do this. I feel this is what God wants me to do. The human needs and demands are unestimable and unmeetable outside of Christ. I try to feed, care for and protect the flock I am called to shepherd and to train others to do so too. Training and equipping of local leadership is vital if the church is to thrive. I can't really see that I am trying to do anything different from other pastors, ministers and leaders in the area. I am only as gifted, equipped and anointed as God makes me—and so the onus is on God. I am saved by God's grace and also minister in his grace. There is surely no real difference between the call I feel and the call male Christian pastors feel?

The day-by-day experience of my work seems to overlap constantly rather than diverge from the experience of other Christian ministers in the area. We have few difficulties in sharing our call, concerns, joys and problems. To be honest, I'm rarely aware that differences of approach are determined by anything other than theology, personality or experience and it is hard to label a specifically male or female style of working. It is, of course, true that sexuality is an integral part of our make-up: we are all male and female. We work with and respond to people who are male and female. This for me draws us to the conclusion that our leadership teams should comprise both men and women. This togetherness is part of the expression of the divine image in the redeemed society.

Ministry in East London has been to me a whole-life experience. Our church life produces in our lives a degree of structure and pattern focusing in and flowing out from Sunday worship and teaching together. There is increasingly, for some, times of prayer and Bible study each day. No one it seems can stop the daily upheavals of life from protruding into our days. Ministry may include praying for the healing of the sick or unblocking a toilet, breaking into a flat to rescue the victim of a fall or teaching on evangelism, but it's still ministry. We are trying to bring the word of God and to show the love of Christ in every situation. My days are very varied. I have wrestled with people's corsets, discussed pregnancies and family life, prayed for jobs for people, led open-air witness in the market and chaired meetings. Without too much cliché I can say I've split my sides laughing and hurt my eyes crying—but that's life!

Those in leadership and ministry are surely meant to call and enable others to follow Jesus Christ. Scripture is dotted with examples of women who have done this. History will speak of many women and men who are doing this now. If we hope, work and pray for a growth of the church in England in the last decade of the twentieth century, then leadership must be a key element of our requests to God.

'Lord Jesus pour out your Spirit on all people—even on your servants, both men and women, that they may lead your church. And everyone who calls on the name of the Lord will be saved. Amen.'

7

Pioneer in a Man's World

by

Vivienne Faull

Vivienne Faull is chaplain of Gloucester Cathedral

In retrospect it is significant that it was years before I could begin to think of becoming an Anglican minister. It ought to have been obvious to me and to others. My parents were closely involved in an Anglican parish and we all went to church. We didn't grumble much because the Sunday school was fun and as we grew older we realised that church was the centre for gossip and entertainment in the village. Our home was a place where faith was taken seriously, and while bringing up their four young children, our parents were thinking deeply about their own vocation. That thinking would eventually lead my mother from the task of leading the Sunday school into training as a reader, and my father from singing in the choir to non-stipendiary ordained ministry.

I was educated at Church of England schools. The vicar came once a week to take assembly in our infant class and that worship brought together the two things I loved: words and music. The *English Hymnal* taught me words which were not in my reading books, and tunes which were better than the ones in my recorder book. I sang that God was immortal, invisible and inaccessible and that I believed firmly that God was Three and God was One. Once a week we listened to the School Service on the radio. Before each service the announcer put on a record by a composer called 'Bark'. I enjoyed that very much.

Some months later the family moved from Berkshire to Cheshire. In my new village school we were tested each day on our tables and then our recitation of the Shorter Catechism. I learned more interesting long words. I moved on to secondary school and was encouraged to develop my musical interests. I sang and played in local churches, most of them much more beautiful than our own parish church, the worship continuing to attract me. Other aspects of church life held me. Some school friends had set up a prayer group. We met informally as an extension of one of the city church youth groups. Living out in the village it was exciting to meet with other people of my age. Going to a girls' school, it was even more exciting to meet boys. And we did pray, for ourselves, the church and for the world; though we spent a long time getting ready to pray.

We were an academic bunch of kids. By the time I reached the sixth form I was thinking hard about some of the religious concepts I had learned as a child. My headmistress encouraged me to apply to Oxford to read Theology. I pompously thought that too easy a way in and applied to read History.

The next three years were to help me hear God's calling, though I hesitated to discern the nature of that call. Before going to Oxford I spent nine months as a member of the Lee Abbey community of Christians working in their hostel for students from overseas who had come to London. Little more than a naive schoolgirl, I found the cleaning I did physically exhausting and the culture of Earls Court utterly disorientating, but with the support of the community I thrived. It was a delight to be able to integrate my faith and my work. For the first time I felt as if I were taking Christianity seriously. I had the rather romantic idea of forgetting university and committing myself to the community for the rest of my life. Fortunately, I was encouraged to move on.

Oxford was stretching. It took me a while to find my academic and social balance. Church life became increasingly important. At St Aldate's I encountered enthusiasm and numbers as I had never imagined possible in the Church of England. And for the first time I encountered women working as ministers, St Aldate's having recently employed two women in their twenties as lay pastors. By my final year several of my friends were considering going on to theological training. Many had been encouraged by college chaplains or by church staff. I was rather envious that there was such an obvious way for them to offer their lives in God's service. I went off to the university careers service and thought about becoming a lawyer.

There were several reasons why I was not encouraged to consider ministry. Apart from the two women working in short-term jobs in an Oxford church, I had met no women ministers. Indeed at that point there were very few women paid workers, so I had no model to adopt. The clergy at Oxford knew how to encourage men to follow in the path they themselves had taken, but few of them were aware of opportunities available to women. In addition, some of them were struggling with the biblical texts which seemed to encourage women into subordinate and domestic roles.

My parents had invested considerable amounts of emotion and money in my education and expected me to establish myself in a career. In the early 1970s women had to be parish workers for several years before they could be considered for admission to the order of deaconess. Parish workers had little job security, inadequate housing provision, few opportunities to take on posts of responsibility and poor pension rights. I was not aware of this. My mother was. She did not suggest that I should consider paid church work.

At the beginning of my final year, however, there was a change. Students had been encouraged into leadership at church. I joined a group of friends in a rock band. What we lacked in skill we made up for in noise. We were dreadful, but still got invitations to schools and church youth groups to play and to talk about our faith. In September we spent a week away from Oxford on a mission to a group of parishes in Manchester. I enjoyed the work in schools and among

young people immensely, but when one night we were asked
to go and talk to the women out working on the streets of
Moss Side, I retreated to the pub. The leader of our section of
the mission team, a clergyman then working for the Church
Pastoral Aid Society, sat down beside me. We probably had
a long conversation. All I remember now were his words:
'Viv, you are going to be a deaconess.'

My response was curiously ambivalent, partly delighted
at his words of affirmation, partly angry at his presumption.
He said little more, other than insisting that I took his words
seriously. I promised that I would and spent the next few
weeks sounding out my friends. I was sent to the Oxford
Diocesan Lay Ministry Advisor, who sent me on to the
Chester equivalent who eventually unearthed a committee
of very elderly clergymen who eventually agreed that I
should be allowed to 'test my vocation at a conference
organised by the Advisory Council for the Church's Ministry'.

Shortly after Easter 1977 I found myself at such a conference, along with fifteen other women and several selec-
tors. By this stage I was becoming rather fearful about what
I might be taking on. Ruth Wintle, secretary of that conference, told us that there was now a possibility that we
might be licensed as deaconesses as soon as we finished
training. I was not sure that I had met a deaconess apart
from Ruth, who is a wise, attractive and witty woman, and
suddenly I was seized with the idea that if I became a
deaconess I would have to become dowdy, sensible and
solemn.

I was recommended for theological training and immediately asked Ruth if I could take a couple of years to explore
other possibilities. A month after graduation I flew to India
to teach English at a school run by the Church of North
India in Bihar. Eighteen months later I flew back to do youth
and community work, funded by unemployment benefit, in
Everton. By that time I had done enough running away and
I started to apply to theological colleges.

There has been considerable debate about training for
women in the Church of England. There are fewer women
than men entering theological college and at the moment
they are not training for identical jobs. This raises questions
about the location and nature of courses. There are those
who emphasise the importance of women to be trained as
cohorts rather than as individuals, giving them the strength
of numbers both to support one another adequately and to
influence the masculinity of the training institution. This
theory requires that women be offered places at a restricted
number of institutions.

Then there are those who emphasise the significance of
ensuring that male ordinands train alongside women, learning over the months how to work with them as colleagues.
This theory requires that women be spread through all the
different institutions, perhaps in small numbers. There are
those who believe that, since women's and men's roles in the
church are different, their training should be different. And
there are those who are working for women's and men's roles
in the church to be interchangeable who believe that their
training should be identical.

In 1978 there were fourteen residential theological colleges in England training Anglican ordinands. Five were
permitted by the central church authorities to train women.
Having studied at Oxford, I was used to being in a minority,
and argued that once I began work for the church I would
expect once again to be in a minority. Having read history I
was aware that a different training could easily be perceived
as an inferior training, and argued that I should have the
same freedom of application as the men. I applied to two
colleges at that stage not permitted to accept women candidates. My applications were rejected. I argued the case at
Church House Westminster, and lost. I then applied to St
John's Nottingham, where Colin Buchanan, then acting
Principal, agreed to argue my case. Twelve months later I
was finally given permission to go to Nottingham.

Nowadays all but one of the fourteen colleges admit
women, though the debate about the nature of their train-

ing continues both within the colleges and at General
Synod.

There were three parts to my training, two formal and one
informal. I was delighted to have time to study theology and
began to wrestle with some of the questions I had stored up
for years. The Nottingham University degree gave me the
basis for honest questioning. The college teaching gave me a
framework within which I could construct provisional
answers. Above all, the enthusiasm, generosity and ability of
the college lecturers gave me an unfailing love for the task of
doing theology. I could not be more grateful.

The other formal part of the course was in effect the
practical application of theology, from preaching to prayer,
from counselling to evangelism. St John's was one of the first
Anglican colleges to take pastoral studies seriously and its
contacts in a variety of professional disciplines and its own
large staff enabled it to offer a great range of well-supervised
experiences.

In my last year I spent two days a week in a lively parish in
Loughborough where I was given responsibility for the
young people's confirmation class as well as considerable
scope for leading worship. It was reassuring to discover that
I enjoyed parish work, and that a parish which had not
encountered a woman in ministry previously could apparently take to one without a murmur.

The informal part of the training, the hidden curriculum,
was equally formative. I found that at 7.45am I could cope
with liturgical prayer but not a praise service. Living in a
cell-like room on a corridor with twelve other ordinands felt
like a repetition of my other experiences of community life. I
was elected president of the student body and discovered
that I enjoyed politics no end.

For many people theological training can be profoundly
disturbing. For me it was profoundly healing. It gave me the
chance to begin to live with the hurts of Oxford and India.
It gave me the reassurance that it was not mad or bad to
feel called to ministry. It gave me the reassurance that

it was not mad or bad as a woman to feel called to be ordained. It made me glad to be a Christian and hopeful for the Church of England. The next task was to find a job.

I wrote to Chester diocese. I was sent a list of incumbents and told to write to all of them saying that they could have me as long as they could find the money to pay me. This did not seem an ideal arrangement, so I got permission to look elsewhere. I was asked to look at two tiny Leicester villages with very grand Lords of the manor, then at an urban parish in Southwark where the vicar seemed on the point of collapse, then a large church with an evangelical emphasis where there would have been no opportunity for a woman worker to preach, or lead worship, then a couple of parishes in Liverpool.

Increasingly, Liverpool felt like home. Frances Briscoe, the Diocesan Lay Ministry advisor realised that, discovered that the diocese was going to be allowed to employ additional assistant staff, and arranged for a job to be created for me at Mossley Hill Parish Church, a couple of miles south of the city centre. I was ordained deaconess in the cathedral at Michaelmas 1982.

Mossley Hill was an ideal place to start work. The vast Victorian church had been well restored after second world war bombing. The Father Willis organ had survived, the stained glass fragments had been refashioned by Carl Edwards, who worked in Liverpool Cathedral, into great East and West windows. The vicar, Ken Riley, when university chaplain, had suggested that since most of the Halls of Residence were in the parish, it should become, at least informally, the university church. He was invited by the diocese to become vicar himself. During his ministry there, with his particular gifts as a liturgist and preacher, the church filled with people and life and a whole range of ages and traditions were drawn together.

Ken prepared the way for me carefully. Before I arrived, he obtained a unanimous vote from the PCC in favour of employing a woman staff member. Then he explained what my role would be. 'Lady Vicar for Mossley Hill?' was the headline in the parish magazine, and, in typical scouse fashion, that was how I was welcomed when I went visiting. When I arrived he gave me lots of space, put up with my energy and enthusiasm, was honest about his own faith and ministry and was unfailingly supportive. The people of the parish trained me. It was a place where people prayed, read their Bibles and talked about their faith. They welcomed me, laughed at me, showed me how a parish works and knocked me into the shape that seemed to fit.

Mossley Hill had the advantage of being in Liverpool diocese. Clergy morale was high. In the city of Josephine Butler and Eleanor Rathbone women had established themselves as lay leaders. Dss Thelma Tomlinson had worked in the diocese from 1969 to ensure that women in ministry were recognised and supported by the hierarchy. Indeed, our male colleagues often said that under Frances Briscoe, her successor, women were better cared for than they were. Certainly the thirty or so women and layworkers under Frances' care created a strong support group.

As everywhere, the ordination of women was beginning to be discussed seriously. There were many opponents, but the debate was essentially respectful. In early 1983 I asked that the anniversary of my ordination might be marked in some way, since the men who had been ordained with me would then be priested. The bishop agreed that I should be invited to process, should sit near those to be priested, and that a suitable prayer would be included for me in the service. It became a poignant event. The woman who had been ordained with me the year before felt she could not join the procession because she was working as a non-stipendiary assistant in an Anglo-Catholic parish where she had little support.

The passing of the Peace after the ordination was clearly going to be a difficult time for us all. The stress was reduced because of a nice piece of logistical wit. When I reached the front of the cathedral I realised that the diocesan officials had decided that if I couldn't sit with the ordinands I should sit with the bishops' wives.

When I left theological college I was not sure that I felt called to priesthood. A year in the parish made me certain that I was. This became obvious during my second year. Ken left the parish to join the cathedral staff. The churchwardens were technically in charge, but their normal administrative responsibilities were considerable and they handed to me responsibility for worship and pastoral care.

The main service on Sunday was communion. Some of the time the university chaplain was available, but during the vacations I had to look elsewhere. One Sunday the only priest available warned me that he would have to arrive late and leave early. I suspect he was making a point. He succeeded. That afternoon members of the congregation rang me one after another. 'Viv, you're our vicar, why can't you take the service?' Increasingly people were treating me as a priest. I could and did take baptisms and funerals. Most people thought that entirely appropriate, since women still have so much responsibility in our culture at times of birth and death, joy and grief. If there was an objection I would always hand the task on. The neighbouring clergy were supportive and helpful, and the rural dean was surprised that there were so few objections. The undertakers told me that increasingly people were coming to them asking for deaconesses to take funerals. I asked why. They said they were often told that the women 'do it better'. I suspect that was partly because women were taking more time and trouble; they were still new to the task and trying hard. It was also that because they were women and seen to be more approachable than their male colleagues, they often dis- covered more about the family and made the service more personal.

However, women are as prone as men to funeral disasters. Once, halfway through the first hymn, I saw a furry tail wagging far at the back of the church. My cat had found her way in. She made her way to the front, round the coffin, up into the pulpit and on up to the high altar. I knew that if I chased her the service would disintegrate, so I pretended not to notice her. Later, at the cemetery, I apologised. They didn't seem to mind, even though their grandmother hadn't particularly liked cats. And they gave me a little extra for the church funds.

The gap between vicars can be a very good time in a parish. That was true for us. Members of the congregation stopped asking for help and started giving it. They stopped waiting for the clergy to do everything and got on with it themselves. We prepared together for the visit of Billy Graham. We visited every home in the parish. One Roman Catholic couple told us that of course they were coming to Anfield. We had been to see their Pope when he came to Liverpool, so of course they must come to see ours. Fifty of the congregation volunteered to train as counsellors. It was very moving to watch them down on the turf, talking to complete strangers night after night about being a Christian.

That autumn David Wills arrived as vicar. Assistant staff are dependent on their incumbents for their jobs. Women employed in Anglican parishes are in law, at the moment, always assistants. Their jobs are never secure. One little girl articulated my vulnerability very accurately. She asked her mother, 'Doesn't Viv have to leave now?'

'No,' her mother replied, 'why do you think so?'

'Hasn't she got to go and run another interregnum?'

After a few months of working with David it was clear that he wanted to take the parish in new directions and that I would be hankering after the old ones. It was time to move on. Once again I began job hunting, this time with the aid of the back pages of the *Church Times*. Several people pointed out one particular advertisement, for a chaplain at Clare College Cambridge. I applied and was called for interview. Not knowing my way around, I walked into a college porters' lodge, assuming the college was Clare, and said, 'I have come for an interview for the chaplain's job.' Some months later the chaplain of St John's reminded me that I had tried to oust him. I arrived in Cambridge late in September 1985, realising that such jobs usually went to academic men from Oxbridge theological colleges and wondered if I or the college had made a dreadful mistake.

Clare was founded in the fourteenth century by Elizabeth, Lady Clare who was concerned that plague had reduced the number of men available to serve in high office in church and state. It was soon overshadowed by its neighbouring royal foundations, King's and Trinity. Its ecclesiastical members were middling folk, the exceptions including Hugh Latimer, who was burned during the Marian persecutions, Nicholas Ferrar who, with his household, created the first post-reformation religious community at Little Gidding, and Thomas Merton, whose unhappy year in the college was to set him on the path towards the contemplative religious life.

In the 1960s the college was rescued from mediocrity by its fellowship, which decided to admit students not on the basis of class or gender, but academic ability. In 1972 Clare was among the first Cambridge colleges to admit women. Since 1975 it has been at or near the top of the Cambridge academic league table. Ten years later it was the first college to appoint a woman as chaplain.

I was given a succinct job description. I was to assist the Dean, Rowan Williams, in the conduct of worship in chapel, to have oversight of the pastoral care of the junior members of the college and to contribute to the well-being of the college community. The chapel, a small eighteenth-century building tucked away at the front of the college, still attracted a large minority of students to a variety of services.

I realised that my own student experience had not taught me how to pray. A group of us met sleepily each morning to learn together. The chapel choir of men and women led Evensong three times a week and broadcast frequently. We were the first major chapel choir to 'go mixed' and begin to subvert the conservatism of church music. I was the first woman to sing Evensong on Radio 3, but I am still waiting for some responses to be written especially for a woman precentor to sing. Under Rowan's successor, Nick Sagovsky, we introduced a termly family service. Some of the fellows and staff brought their children, which gave us all an excuse for drama, songs and craftwork. The chapel began to emerge as a lively community of all generations.

My pastoral responsibilities stretched way beyond the chapel community. A colleague described his college as a village with a vastly overgrown youth group. As in any village the boundaries between 'Christian' and 'non-Christian' were blurred. I was available to anyone as a friend or advocate, and spent most of my time with people who had no contact with chapel. I felt as much of a missionary as I had done in India. I worked particularly as a counsellor, supplementing the role of the overstretched University Counselling Service. In a college with high expectations it was inevitable that there would be a high level of stress. It emerged that that stress was compounded by Government policy on higher education. Everyone, from the Master down to the most junior undergraduate, felt under pressure to prove themselves. For women students and fellows there was still greater pressure on them, as still a minority, to make their mark on the institution.

I decided that I must work particularly among the women, supporting individuals and groups and working to make sure they had proper access to places of power. I began to write on women's issues, to call myself a feminist and to take a high profile on church debates. I lobbied for the revision of the *Alternative Service Book* to use language which made women visible; after being made deacon I was elected to General Synod to represent women in the House of Clergy; I sat on the committee which revised the legislation which, if passed, will allow women to be ordained priests.

My ordination to the diaconate in Ely Cathedral in 1987, which felt like a low-key repeat of my initial ordination in 1982, did bring one big change to my work. It was now legal for me to take weddings. When I began work in Liverpool Helena Prince, who had been a deaconess since 1966, said that her desire was not to be allowed to preside at the eucharist, but to be allowed to marry those she had baptised.

In Clare weddings were great fun because I had time to work with the couple so they could express themselves in the service, and facilities for music and catering which eased the task of preparation. We dealt with all sorts of situations: marriages where parents disapproved, marriages with ten attendants under eight, bilingual wedding services, non-patriarchal wedding services, marriage after co-habitation (most of them), marriage after divorce, the marriage of the grandfather of one of our undergraduates, a service of blessing for a Roman Catholic and a Hindu, and a service with four best men, two bride's fathers and a congregation which included six sex therapists.

Over five years my role within the college and university expanded. In my second year I took the funeral of a graduate student who had AIDS. My concern for him and his family led me to encourage the college to consider how it might take responsibility for AIDS education. The university and the Health Authority soon became involved and Cambridge is now at the forefront of innovative work with young adults at risk. The Clare College Students' Committee presented me with a condom case as a memento of the campaign. Inevitably, such work led me into work with the Gay and Lesbian community, especially among couples who had to keep their relationships secret and among Christians who had to keep their sexual orientation secret.

Five years at Clare made me think hard about the pressures of ministry in a job which was seen as glamorous and in which I was seen as successful, and yet which often felt stressful and lonely. As a chaplain there was the pressure of responsibility for vulnerable adults and the challenge of being a very exposed Christian among very shrewd atheists. As a woman there was the strain of needing to prove that a woman could 'do it'. When once I was misquoted in the local newspaper on a particular ethical debate, there were plenty of letters telling me that my comments illustrated how women couldn't and shouldn't. I felt I must not show

how much those letters hurt, for fear of proving their point.

At the moment there is little support for the few women in such exposed places. The risk is that we hide the hurt we experience until we explode, and are blamed for being fragile, or we hide the hurt we experience until we are no longer sensitive to it, and are blamed for being hard. I know that without the support of chaplains from other colleges, my five years at Cambridge could have been very damaging indeed.

And so, at the end of a five-year contract, I was back on the job market, wanting very much to be allowed to be a vicar, knowing that was impossible. Again, I looked fairly widely and have recently taken a job, newly created, as Chaplain of Gloucester Cathedral. I have particular responsibility for visitors and for the pastoral care of the congregation. Once again I can combine the liturgical and the pastoral with a missionary task. Once again I am in an environment where prayer matters. Once again, it ought to have been an obvious next move. But it still feels like another of God's surprises.

8

Breaking the Stereotypes

by

Teresa M Rutterford

Teresa Rutterford is a Methodist minister on the South Shields circuit, in Tyne and Wear

'Will Peter be Mummy then?' This is a sample of just one of the comments which I received at one of the many interviews during the 'candidating' procedure for acceptance into the Methodist ministry. The questioner will remain in my memory for a long time because of his amazing, if not rude, enquiry. Poor man! It seemed then, as it still does today, a tragedy that a man apparently cannot care for his children without being regarded as 'a mother'; as if a father does not get involved in their love and care without losing his masculinity! At the time, my response to this particular comment was unsympathetic and short (the questioner was both young and well educated, and could easily have phrased it differently if he had wanted to!); but other comments were responded to far more gently by me, especially when they were made by elderly, male ministers who had come into our ministry many years ago when those in training were not only male but had to remain unmarried until after ordination! It was at least understandable, even if not acceptable, that they needed to find ways of comprehending how someone in my family situation could manage in full-time ministry.

From a lady in one church came a question about how I would cope with two jobs at the same time, by which she meant looking after the family and being a minister. I did not answer her immediately, but gently enquired about her own life activities. After insisting that she did not work, but spent all her time looking after her home, her husband and her two children, she then went on to tell me that she belonged to several organisations, that she held office in many of them, was responsible for the organising of numerous events, worked for voluntary groups, and that very often she did not seem to have one single evening during the week to call her own! I told her that I thought I was very fortunate to have only two jobs.

So what is our family situation? And how have my husband and I managed our domestic arrangements? Let me begin by saying that Peter, my husband, has worked in the field of computer programming and systems analysis for several years, and he is at present also training as a local preacher in the Methodist Church. When I began candidating in March 1986 our three sons were aged twelve years, nine years and twenty-one months. Our eldest son, Francis, is now seventeen years old (and taking driving lessons); Jerome is fourteen years old (and looking towards choosing his options for GCSEs); and Toby, the youngest, is six years old.

The last thing I expected, in 1986, was that I would be applying for the full-time ministry at that or any other point in my life, especially as our lives were full, comfortable and happy. A couple of years before this, in 1984, we had been planning on moving from our home in East Anglia to Cheshire where Peter had begun a new job for a company there as an analyst programmer. Peter had hardly been there three months when, quite literally overnight, he was made redundant. The company gave him and the others on the computer side only four hours' notice! As a family we were plunged overnight into the situation which so many other people have had to face. Even the fact that we had not sold our house in Norfolk, so at least we had somewhere to live, was cold comfort. We had a family to provide for, bills to pay and mortgage payments to meet. We had no savings to draw on and no income apart from a small amount from my part-time job in a local school's Special Unit. There was only one thing which remained the same in our lives, and that was our faith. But it still was not an easy experience, and it made us work out what was really essential to us and what we could do without.

This, although I did not realise it at the time, was partly responsible for my present situation—not, I hasten to say, because we needed a secure income! Apart from the fact that ministers are notoriously overworked and underpaid, Peter actually got a job again very quickly and our financial situation was soon resolved. No, what Peter's redundancy did was to make me look at the depth of my faith and commitment over a period of about the two years which followed. During this time I gradually became more aware of being drawn towards a full-time commitment to the church.

However, the fact remained that I was a mother of a still young family, and apart from my own job, my husband was in a line of work with career prospects. How could I ask him to support me in a way of life which would completely disrupt his? It needs to be remembered that the Methodist ministry is itinerant; that while we have a certain amount of choice in our later appointments, the first appointment (or 'stationing') is made by our governing body: the conference. Also, every Methodist minister is under the discipline of the conference which has authority to station, or move, a minister to an appointment at any time. While this does not happen frequently, and conference tries not to disrupt ministers and families without good cause, it does nevertheless happen often enough for us to have to accept that it may affect us.

I was therefore quite content to think that at some point in the future, as and when the time was right, the door would be opened for me to go towards the full-time ministry, but for now at least I would continue happily as I was. Little did I suspect what was going to happen next!

Quite out of the blue, in 1985, Peter suddenly turned to me one evening as we relaxed watching television, and suggested that I ought seriously to consider entering the full-time ministry. As I had never spoken about it to anyone, this

came as a complete surprise. I had been so sure that my
calling would be an impossible imposition on Peter that I
had not even considered discussing it with him. Yet here he
was, telling me that he felt it was something I ought to be
thinking about.

So it was from this position of encouragement and support
from Peter that my application went forward, and it made a
big difference knowing that my partner was willingly supportive; for this is something we all need in ministry, both
females and males, if we have a partner who is with us. But it
would be both wrong and naive to claim that being a
woman—a mother of a still young family—made no difference to the attitudes of those who interviewed, voted and
held responsibility for the decisions regarding whether I was
to be accepted or not. There were times when the set
attitudes of individuals were very much to the fore; times
when it was clear that for particular people a woman's role
revolved most naturally around motherhood, family and
domestic concerns. At times these attitudes caused great
frustration to me, belonging, as they do, more to the realms
of popular romantic literature or television 'soaps' where
women are often pigeonholed into cosy domestic roles, over-
emotional 'reactive' roles, bossy and overbearing roles, or
depicted as 'nervy', dependent creatures! And none of these
roles fitted me! Anyone would have found these attitudes
annoying—all beliefs which pay little attention to the facts
cause us similar frustrations. Admittedly there are women
who do seem to fit into these kinds of caricatures without too
much trouble; but so do many men! Such attitudes are
difficult, because they ignore the gifts, character, thoughts
and responses of us as individuals, and see us only as
genders.

Such attitudes place particular pressures and expectations on a man as well, irrespective of whether he is married
or single, as they logically require him to be strong, steady,
masterful, protective and able to support and provide for a
wife and children if he has them. This perception of the
different roles of men and women is not an uncommon one,

and while they may be the chosen roles for many, it is not reasonable to impose them on all. For, just as some women's lives are damaged, denied and unfulfilled because they cannot live and conform to traditional patterns, so also are many men unhappy in the lifestyles into which they feel society has locked them.

Some of the attitudes towards me, as a woman candidating for the church's ministry, especially one with a husband and three children, were both rigid and oppressive, showing little acknowledgement for my humanity, but a great deal of interest in my duties as a wife and mother; an acknowledgement withheld from other candidates who were husbands and fathers! One man, for instance, who was candidating at the same time as myself, had children as I did, and was married as I am. While I was questioned at great length on the care of my children—arrangements for their supervision, meals, and so on—he was not shown the same degree of concern for his family's provision. While I was questioned, at great length once more, about my husband's response to my call to enter the ministry—how this would affect his job, his career, his willingness to move around the country—my male counterpart's wife was not given this same depth of concern. The assumption was that his wife would be at home looking after the children, would be happy to do so, and content to move wherever her husband was stationed!

Even in Methodism, where women candidates have been accepted into the ministry for over fifteen years, we still have much more to learn about the need to see one another primarily as human beings—as God's creation, loved and accepted, called to service by him—rather than the common view of: 'Male: therefore breadwinner, provider; female: therefore dependent and subservient.'

It might be helpful to describe some of the practical aspects of the Methodist 'candidating' procedure. 'Candidating' is the application by an individual to enter the church to be trained as a minister. It is a lengthy process, taking about eighteen months from the initial acceptance from one's own local circuit churches to entering theological college, or some other specified training scheme, if accepted by the Methodist conference. All ministers are under the discipline of the conference, and it is the conference that appoints them to serve in local churches and circuits for a period of five years. (This period of time in an appointment can be altered by mutual agreement between minister, circuit church representatives and conference.) Most Methodist ministers are itinerant, although the pattern of ordained ministry is changing. The 'circuit' is the name given to the group of churches locally which relate to, and work with, one another. The circuits within certain geographical boundaries then join together to form larger entities called 'districts', and the 'connexion' is the word we use to describe the whole of Methodism throughout the country.

During the time I was candidating we lived in a town in Norfolk called Downham Market. It was a strenuous time for us all, because no matter how well each interview or examination went, the final decision could only be made at the conference which met two or three months prior to the start of training for an accepted candidate. During this period of testing and examination we all, as a family, received support and encouragement, both practical and spiritual. It was also a time when again, as a family, we looked even more closely at the kinds of changes such a calling would bring about for us individually. Peter was totally convinced of the rightness of my calling, and his support throughout has been essential. Even on occasions when the strain of uncertainty has been difficult to bear, the overwhelming conviction that this was God's calling to us served to smooth stressful situations which arose—but we still had to work hard ourselves as we adjusted to the new patterns which a life of ministry was forming within our lives.

I would not want to emphasise one kind of attitude shown by those who interviewed, without making mention of others. Many men and women on the various panels and committees who saw each candidate, did take us on our own merits. The majority were much more concerned with whether we had a true calling and commitment than whether we were female or male. Most wanted to ask questions concerned with discovering the fitness of each candidate for a life of ordained ministry. So while some of those interviewing gave a strong impression that any woman in the ministry ought to be either single or old enough to have grown up children (or perhaps even with a husband who was old enough to take early retirement and look after the family!), the majority by far were quite different: encouraging, open-hearted, open-minded, interested and concerned.

After being unanimously accepted as a minister in training, I then began two years of study at Wesley House, Cambridge, beginning in September 1987. First of all, we were the first family not to live in the college, nor even in Cambridge itself, while at the same time being classed as 'full-time residential'. We remained in our home in Downham Market in order that Peter could continue to work and supplement my grant, and so that the boys could continue with their schooling. Francis was about to begin his GCSEs, so it would have been hard for us to move just then. Also, we faced a further move into circuit after the two years of my training, which would have been doubly disruptive. It worked out quite well for all of us: as well as keeping Peter and the two older boys in the continuity of work and school, Toby was able to attend a local full-time nursery and we had the back up of family and long-standing friends. One good friend, Lorraine, looked after Toby and Jerome at home after school, and was more like a family member to all of us. And a neighbour who had long ago been adopted into the family as 'Auntie Pearl', was marvellous in the way she stepped in to help if we needed it.

As for myself, I commuted daily to Cambridge by train and bicycle. I had to cycle to the station each morning, leaving Peter to take Toby to nursery (Jerome and Francis were old enough to get to school on their own—especially as they only had to go down the road to reach it!). Then I had to put my bicycle in the guard's van, take it out at Cambridge and cycle through Cambridge to the college. At the end of the day I reversed the whole procedure to come home. It meant leaving the house by about 7.40am, and the journey took something like an hour in total. It certainly kept me fit and made me find out a bit more about bicycle maintenance! But it was not so good when the weather was bad. I remember being caught in many downpours, as well as battling against terrible gales at the end of 1987 when I had left the house earlier than usual and had not heard the weather warnings; I was caught out in the winds on my bicycle in Cambridge with rubbish bins flying at me and branches falling around me. It was very frightening! I remember, too, the first couple of weeks at the beginning of this commuting: I had an old, heavy-framed bicycle, and when I started my training, it felt as if I would collapse by the time I had pedalled up even the gentlest of slopes! I had not ridden for years, and I soon traded in my old, heavy bicycle for a new, lightweight one. It did not even matter that it took a great chunk out of my first term's grant—it was worth every penny not to arrive red faced, sweaty and breathless! Two friends and I even cycled all the way from Cambridge to Downham Market on Red Nose Day in 1989, raising nearly £400 for Comic Relief. Whoever said that theological training was sedentary or dull!

The children's school holidays were not difficult either, as the college vacations were the same time and were usually even longer than the school breaks. I usually tried to do my studying during the day before returning home at tea time, so that I could break off then and relax with my family. It did not always work out that way: sometimes the older boys had their own arrangements for seeing friends in the evenings, sometimes Peter had his own meetings to go to, and there were occasions when I had to burn the midnight oil at home to get my work done.

Within the Methodist Church our training also involves us in the leading of worship and preaching on Sundays in our churches. All candidates applying for our ministry will have had to have been local preachers in circuits, and will have taken many services during their training and examinations in local preaching. During ministerial training the preaching continued, so that there were even weekends when I could not be with my family because of preaching commitments, often many miles away. However, this had been such a normal way of life of us, with both Peter and me as local preachers, that it made no real difference. Indeed, prior to my training at Cambridge, I had been conducting services every fortnight to three weeks, and during my training I was actually required to preach less rather than more! One of the main reasons why we coped so well, apart from wanting to support one another as best we could, was because we went into all of this with our eyes open. We expected there to be difficulties at times, so when they came they did not throw us off balance—all, that is, except once. . . .

We are exceptionally fortunate in that we have all kept good health, or if we are ill we tend just to carry on rather than go into an immediate state of self-pity or collapse! But during my training, in the summer between my first and second year, our eldest son was taken ill. At first he did not say how bad he was feeling, and insisted that he needed no special attention. But eventually we persuaded him to come to the doctor's surgery, where he was told he had tonsilitis and was given some antibiotics. Within two days he had collapsed, was completely covered in a terrible skin rash and could hardly breathe. I was on placement at the time, working alongside ministers in a nearby circuit. When I arrived home to find Francis in such a state I was shocked, and was not helped by a friend who criticised me for not being at home earlier. The doctor came straight round and we took Francis to hospital. He actually had glandular fever and the antibiotics had been the cause of his rash and side-effects.

I realised during all of this that the pulls a minister feels between the needs of church members and the needs of his or her own family are tremendous. I also realised that the criticism I received from my friend was not to do with being a minister, but to do with being a working mother. My proper place, it seemed to her, should have been at home, and this was made very plain to me. Under the circumstances, though, if she had given me half a chance, I could not have agreed with her more! While it was not necessary for me to be at home every minute, at this time Francis particularly needed me, and no matter what other commitments I had, his need was greatest. Once more, I had had to work out where my priorities lay, but it was a dramatic way of finding out. It worked out very well in the end, though, because while he was in hospital there was little point in my remaining at home, but because part of my training placement was working at the hospital as a chaplain, it meant that I could visit him anytime which suited my schedule. Francis was quite pleased to discover a benefit from the job his mother did!

None of the children have ever been embarrassed to admit that their mother is a minister. To them it seems as right and normal as it does to me. Even now that I am working in circuit and my job takes me into their schools, as well as into Francis' college as both chaplain and a governor, they have no problems admitting to their friends that I am their mother. Once, when Toby was told that ministers were men, he replied with absolute disdain that if you thought that you must be 'completely stupid', and proudly informed the person that his mother was a minister! So far, at least, they have not wanted to disown me.

After my training, the circuit I was sent to was decided by a 'stationing committee' and confirmed by our conference. Although Peter and I were interviewed and his work and our family circumstances were taken into account, we knew we were under discipline to go where we were sent—unless there were glaringly obvious reasons why we shouldn't. Our first appointment has been in the North East of England, in South Shields, where I have pastoral responsibility for two churches at the moment, and will have to take on another church next year due to cutbacks in staff by the circuit. In subsequent appointments we have more choice in that circuits will invite us and we can consider which invitation we would most like to accept. A maximum of five invitations can be considered at any one time, and all Methodist ministers move at the same time of year, late August, to begin the year on 1st September. Our initial invitations are for five years, but can be shorter or longer by mutual agreement. However, even though we have an invitation system, some ministers prefer to be stationed directly by the conference throughout their ministry or simply at certain periods during their ministry, and so opt out of the invitation system at these times.

This, I think, is the moment when I must try to set out how our ministry of both men and women works, because unlike some traditions, there is little if anything which differentiates between the ministry of men and women either spiritually or practically. We all (as active ministers) celebrate both word: the preaching of the gospel; and sacrament: presiding at Holy Communion. We all conduct weddings (as the registered authorised person), funerals and baptisms. We all work in chaplaincies where available and appropriate, and we all have pastoral responsibility for particular churches. Any differences which may exist are not dependent on our gender, but on our particular circumstances.

I have often been told that my single, male colleagues receive practical help from church members which female or married ministers do not receive. The attitude, apparently, goes something like this: a married minister can cope because she/he has a partner to look after them and help with the day-to-day running of the home, and likewise a single woman is capable of doing things for herself! Frankly, I have to say that this is not the most common attitude I have found in my work. It is sad that some colleagues have found such a lack of caring and help in these practical areas, but from our experience I would want to sound a note of reassurance: whether male or female, single or married, the situation may change when the next move takes place. There are loving communities as well as difficult ones, just as there are loving people and the odd awkward customer, too! Our church members have shown their love and support for my ministry in both practical and spiritual ways. Even though I was forewarned that the general assumption would be that I would manage the cooking, cleaning, ironing and domestic chores on my own (because they were chores one expected a woman to carry out), the reality was quite different, and accepting offers of help and generosity given in love has been a humbling and heartwarming experience. Over the course of the first year of my present appointment I have found that, generally speaking, people are concerned to help in any area they are able to.

'We know you haven't time to bake,' is a familiar comment I have received, along with a sponge, a quiche, a tray of biscuits or some jam tarts. People have said that they feel that in helping us as a family and reducing our workload in practical areas, they are serving the church by freeing their minister to be able both to work in the community for the kingdom, and to spend time with the family at home (although this time is always too short, no matter what!). The babysitting offers we receive are much appreciated and are badly needed since the rest of our family is so far away from us now that we are in South Shields.

In pastoral matters there has not been resistance to my work because I am a woman; nor has there been any resistance to my preaching. That is not to say that there are not people who have found the message difficult to accept, but only to say that if that has been the case the reason for any lack of response is not primarily to be found in the fact that I am a woman. The same message preached by a man would be equally difficult to accept!

And yet, even as I write these words and read them through, I know that there are still, within the structures of our church, strong feelings of resistance to the idea or possibility of women's 'advancement' or 'promotion' among ministers and laity alike. Let me explain: for many ministers there is a desire to 'climb the ladder' from being a circuit minister to being circuit superintendent, district chairman (or woman—there is one in the country!), and president of the conference (a one-year appointment). Sometimes these positions of responsibility come unsought and are offered because the minister's special gifts are recognised and needed in these jobs. But for some ministers and church members alike, the prospect of women in these roles within the ministry remains a horrifying one.

I remember a comment from a church member in our previous church when I was training. He said to me as I prepared to enter circuit work, 'I don't mind women being ministers—after all we have them as preachers—but I wouldn't feel comfortable sitting under a woman superintendent.' As I looked at his bony knees, the thought crossed my mind, 'No doubt it wouldn't be very comfortable for the superintendent either, in more ways than one!'

But his attitude is not unusual. Women are still very much seen in the home as homemakers with a family; or if they must work, they receive little encouragement if they seek advancement or promotion. Ambition is the realm of the male, or the female who has lost her 'femininity'! If that sounds hard, it is nevertheless the attitude which still prevails among some, and if we ignore it, we will hurt all the more when it meets us face on. The structures of the church are not so different from those of most traditional organisations, departments and ministries where the 'old boys' network' and the 'school tie' dictate those who advance and those who are ignored. There is still a dominant 'it's not what you know, but who you know' syndrome in existence in the church as in any other traditional organisation. As the church's history has been male dominated through the centuries, it is often only through influential men that women can achieve positions of responsibility.

I have been interested to discover that colleagues (ministers), within the Anglican churches in the area where I work, have accepted me as a minister on a par with themselves, but how much of this is due to the fact that I do not pose a threat, being of another denomination, I cannot say for sure.

Very often, when conducting a wedding or funeral service in particular, I have been approached by men attending the services, and the most common remark is, 'You're the first one I've seen!', by which they mean that it's the first service of this kind that they have been to where a woman minister has presided. All, without exception, have responded favourably to this new experience. An Anglican bishop asked me recently about the churches' response to a woman being 'at the helm'. He asked me if people stayed away, withdrew their membership, and generally how they reacted to me. The honest response, when I think carefully, has to be that the answers are seen in increased congregations, increased commitment, increased financial giving and increased membership (confirmation). He further asked about the response from male colleagues. The honest reply to this is that it is very often the people from whom one seeks fellowship and support the most who give the least support and the most resistance, particularly if one is a woman. Very early on in my ministry a colleague made his feelings plain in this. Not only was he negative towards a minister being a woman, he spoke of his disapproval of all working mothers! However, it needs also to be said clearly that while support may not be given easily between colleagues in the normal daily work, when one minister finds himself or herself facing a particular difficulty, all differences are put aside to give help to one another.

The attitudes which I have described here are not concerned with theological debate, biblical argument or church tradition; what most of them are concerned with are personal prejudice and traditional discrimination. The views expressed by my colleague on working mothers were all the more hurtful because of his position in the church, which was one of authority and influence. While such feelings are expressed and accepted so freely by people who could, if they chose, use their position to bring about changes in the hearts and minds of those they meet and work with, then it will be hard for women to exercise their vocational calling to the full. The pity of it is that wherever one goes, one has invariably to begin again to face, understand and overcome the same recurring prejudices—a little like inventing the wheel over and over again!

But above the hurt; above the occasional negative attitude; above those odd individuals who appear to want to dominate those they feel should be subservient; above all these things comes the voice of God, reassuring and strengthening.

We do not enter the ministry because it is easy or comfortable—it is rarely that! We enter it because we are called by God to do his will and follow his direction. The times of pain and anguish should not be allowed to overshadow those moments in ministry when evangelism, healing, restoration and commitment to Jesus have occurred in the lives of those whom we pastor. Indeed, it is often at these moments, when God's work seems to be going well, that something arises which breaks in destructively upon that work. Perhaps, for a woman, this will most commonly occur as discriminatory attitudes which undermine both our ministry and our humanity at the same time. At moments like these we need to be led back time and again to the Scriptures to be reminded of the way Jesus always saw beyond the labels imposed by society, beyond the constraints of the traditions and laws; how he saw into the hearts of the men and women who came to him. Such reminders serve to keep our hearts free from anger or personal antagonism, so that in the worst situation of hurt we face we still respond with love.

'Will Peter be Mummy then?' No, of course not, any more than I could turn round and be Daddy! I have no wish to give up being a woman, nor have I any wish to give up being a Christian, a minister or a human being—these are all things which enrich my relationships within my family and with those in the community.

I do not regret my calling. Sometimes I find myself saying, 'Why me, O Lord?' And always the same answer comes back, 'Because it is you I have called.' That is enough. God's will be done.

9

Growing in Ministry

by

Judith Rose

Judith Rose is Personal Chaplain to the Bishop of Rochester, Diocesan Deacon, and Associate Diocesan Director of Ordinands

They say that the way we are treated in our early years affects the rest of our lives. As a child I do not remember being treated in a special way because I was a girl. I suppose I learned to think of myself as a person who happened to be female.

My chosen profession was farming, which is very largely a man's world, and women who enter do so on the same terms as men, which always seemed quite reasonable to me. It was not until many years later that I was conscious of meeting discrimination because I was a woman. Sadly, I met that discrimination in the church when I found that my abilities and experience were an embarrassment to the church because I was a woman. I still think of myself primarily as a person who is grateful to God for being female. It amazes me even now, that in the eyes of some people in the church, my femininity is more important than my personality and the bundle of gifts and experiences that has made me the person that I am.

It was in the early 1960s that I began to want to serve God in some form of Christian ministry. Having an agricultural background, I thought it would be exciting and useful to become an agricultural missionary. God had very different plans for me. At the time, I was working for the Ministry of Agriculture in Cornwall. I came to realise that God was saying no to missionary work, but my attention was drawn to serving in the ministry in the Church of England. In those days, for a woman this meant becoming a parish worker. This did not sound a very exciting prospect to someone in her twenties. I had never actually met a parish worker; there weren't any in the Truro diocese in those days. I certainly did not want to become one of them, but the call was insistent and eventually I found myself accepted for training. As soon as I had responded to this call, which I believe came from God, I found my attitude changed and I began to look forward to the future. I have never regretted that decision.

My training took me to St Michael's House in Oxford. It was a small women's Bible college. As I had two years for my training, I decided to get as much out of it as possible. As well as the parish worker qualification of an Inter-Diocesan Certificate, I also studied for a London University Diploma in Theology. I found it a great privilege to have two years in which to study the Bible. I became excited about biblical theology, thanks to some superb lectures, especially in the Old Testament. As well as studying theology, we were trained for a pastoral ministry. I remember preparing talks for women's meetings and Sunday school lessons, but cannot remember any sermon preparation, or even expecting that I would ever preach. Parish workers had a very limited liturgical role. I don't think we ever discussed the ordination of women. It was not an issue—at least not for me.

In 1966, I became a parish worker in a large parish in Swindon. The staff consisted of the vicar, two curates and myself. I visited endlessly on my bicycle, I prepared girls for confirmation and I supervised the Sunday school. I was given £10 per year to cover my expenses. I wore a maroon gown and cap when I helped with services and was nicknamed 'Cardinal Wolsey'. My incumbent insisted that the staff were known by their surnames, so I was Miss Rose, or 'Rosie'! I had been there for more than a year when I was asked to speak at a family service. This I did only very occasionally at first, but my preaching career had started.

I spent five busy but happy years in that parish. The role

of women in the church must have been a growing issue, but I was untouched by it. I proudly boasted to Canon Geoffrey Paul, who was later to be my bishop in Bradford, that I would always be happy to take the role of an assistant. With greater wisdom or foresight he replied, 'You wait, my girl, your views will change.'

My quest for theology remained, and in 1971 I went to the London Bible College to study for an external London Bachelor of Divinity degree. I did not know where it would lead but I enjoyed a further two years' study. It was while there that the issue of women's roles in the church began to impinge on me. I knew I had been called into the ministry and had had five years' parish experience. It was an arrogant eighteen-year-old who challenged my vocation. He said that God would not call women into leadership roles because this was forbidden in the Scripture. He acknowledged that God could have used me by saying, 'God can use anything—he once used the jaw bone of an ass.' It was not very tactful, but at least it made me think. I, too, wanted to live by scriptural principles so concluded that the ordination of women must be wrong, and yet I was sure of my vocation. I thought this meant remaining an assistant to a man.

By the time I left the London Bible College, I had laid a sound foundation for my future ministry. I had done five years in a good training parish, and had learned much about pastoral ministry. I had also acquired a working knowledge of theology. These two dimensions prepared me well for the next phase.

In 1973, I was appointed as parish worker to St George's Church, Leeds. Again, I joined a staff of three clergymen. I was now a graduate in theology and, as it happened, was better qualified theologically than any of my three colleagues. The congregation had been told this so had great expectations before I even arrived. I often wonder if I measured up to their initial expectations, especially as I am only five feet tall. I am sure that both stature and gender condition our initial assessment of people much more than we are aware. Paper qualifications are, of course, no guarantee that a Christian minister will be effective, and I, like any other, had to prove my worth as time went by.

I remained at St George's Church for a total of seven-and-a-half years. They were probably the most formative years of my ministry, as latent gifts began to develop. I was asked to preach about once a month which I enjoyed and found very stimulating, especially because the large congregation was so receptive and, at times, critical. The staff team was also stimulating and many principles were thrashed out together and policy decided. Over the years, various projects were worked through (one at a time), for example lay pastoral elders, all-age instruction for Sunday morning services, a telephone ministry and an evangelistic training programme.

It was a great thrill to be sent by the church to study some large and growing churches in America. What impressed me was the American Sunday school which catered for the whole church membership. As a result, I became involved in setting up something similar in the church in Leeds. Through that, I learned a great deal about the principles of adult education and developed my teaching skills with adults. I had the opportunity to try and enthuse others with my own love of biblical theology. One of the greatest rewards for me has been to see young Christians grow in their faith and in their ability to understand it, articulate it and to put it into practice.

As part of the leadership team, I often found myself taking the chair at meetings, and doing so quite naturally. I began to realise that I had leadership gifts, and started thinking about appropriate styles of leadership for a church. It seemed to me that one of the important aspects of being a leader was first to seek God's vision for that church, which means a lot of knee work. Then to convey that vision to the church so that it catches the vision and owns it. Then to work with the church in seeking to fulfil that common vision. The challenge was to put the theory into practice.

In 1975, the question of the ordination of women came before General Synod. In preparation for that the issue was debated at parish and deanery level. Being a woman in Christian ministry, I was asked for my views and the reasons for holding them. I began by saying that I was opposed to the ordination of women because I believed that Scripture forbade women to hold authority over men. In seeking to defend my position, I was now compelled to think more deeply about it, to explore the Scriptures, and read what others had written. I came to realise it was not an issue that could be answered by a few proof texts. It touched significant doctrines such as creation, the Fall, the Incarnation, redemption and the gifts of the Spirit. I came to believe that to be true to the whole of Scripture, I had to change my views and support the ordination of women. This also made more sense of my own vocation and my growing awareness of the gifts of teaching and leadership that I was increasingly exercising.

It was about this time that I became a deaconess. In part, I did this for the benefit of those who did not know what a parish worker was. To have an ecclesiastical title like 'deaconess' helped to define my role. I was also ready for my lifelong commitment to Christian ministry to be recognised. A parish worker only has the title as long as she is employed, but to be a deaconess was to enter an order of ministry for life. So in 1976 I became a deaconess. Looking back on it now, that is probably when I should have been made a deacon had that been possible. A deaconess is in orders but remains a lay person. I had continually to remind enquirers that a deaconess is not a female deacon, and is not in Holy Orders, nor yet in 'Unholy Orders'!

1975 was also the year when the General Synod elections were held. I had not considered standing until a retiring member asked me to do so. Much to my surprise, I found myself elected to the House of Laity representing Ripon diocese. My maiden speech was in 1976, and was about the diaconate. I was re-elected again in 1980. I did not speak often in General Synod, but learned a great deal through my involvement. Having to read the background material kept me abreast of the current issues, and I became more aware of the structures of the Church of England, as well as getting to know some of the notable figures in the church. A great treat in 1975 was to be invited by John Moorman, who was then Bishop of Ripon, to a meal at the House of Lords.

Around about 1980, I began to be aware of the need for senior posts for women in the church. By this time, I was also the diocesan lay ministry adviser, responsible for deaconesses and parish workers in the diocese, and for women enquiring about the ministry. I wrote a brief paper for the Diocesan Board of Ministry about the lack of openings for women with experience, but the issue was not taken seriously. I had also been appointed to the Vocation and Training Committee of the Church Pastoral Aid Society and under their auspices did some limited research on senior posts for women. I wrote to all the dioceses for their views and to about sixty women who had been in the ministry for more than ten years. The results were interesting, and noted, but nothing was done. No one seemed to have any answers or to have the will to find answers. It was to be another ten years before the church would begin to address the issue, and then only after women were ordained to the diaconate. It seems that while women remained laity, the church did not really take them seriously.

This became a significant issue for me personally after I had been in the ministry about twelve years. I had enjoyed my work and had learned a great deal. I had thought carefully about how a church should be led and pastored to enable its members to develop their own ministry and outreach. I felt I had served a long and useful apprenticeship and I was now ready to spread my wings, make my own decisions and take responsibility for my own successes and failures. I began to find myself silently criticising my vicar and thinking that I could have done some things better than he had done them. It was obviously time to move on. The problem was finding a job that would use my gifts and experience. Had I been a man, I would have had the opportunity to become the vicar of a parish, but that was not possible because I was not and could not be ordained priest. Because I enjoyed my ministry at St George's Church and worked well with my vicar, we thought long and hard about how I could be given more responsibility within the team. We considered areas of ministry for which I could take special responsibility. We even considered the vicar being called 'the rector' and developing more extra-parochial interests, and me becoming 'the vicar' of the congregation. There was plenty of goodwill, but such restructuring proved inappropriate. I had to find a challenge elsewhere.

I was also concerned about my motives for wanting more responsibility. Was this selfishness and 'thinking of myself more highly than I ought to think'? Was I becoming ambitious in a way that was inappropriate for someone in Christian ministry? Christian ministry is by definition about service. This lay behind comments which were often heard in church circles in those days about 'these ambitious women who are seeking status'! I noted that such comments were never heard when men curates were wanting to be vicars. For men it was the fulfilment of a vocation, but for women it was called ambition. I was greatly helped in this by a Christian study group which on one occasion looked at the subject of ambition. We decided that ambition was wrong if it meant self-preferment at the expense of others, but that it could be right if it were a matter of seeking to develop and use to the full God-given potential in a way that was helpful rather than harmful to others. As far as I could discern my own motives, that was what I wanted to do.

And so the search for a new appointment began. I followed up numerous openings. Some resulted in interviews which took me to at least eight different dioceses. Some jobs would have offered me less scope than I already had. At other interviews I sensed that I had more experience and initiative than the vicar, and knew that that could lead to difficult relationships. Nothing seemed to open up for me. I began to think seriously that I would have to leave the ministry. I considered joining the Methodist Church who did allow women to become ministers, but it did not seem to be the right reason for changing denominations. This was quite a dark period for me; there seemed to be no way forward, and yet neither had God released me from my vocation.

Eventually, I was invited to join the staff of Bradford Cathedral. Bradford is a parish church cathedral with a large regular eclectic congregation. The provost of the cathedral was a parish priest at heart, having been vicar of a large thriving church before being appointed provost, yet as provost he had responsibility in the city and diocese. In fulfilling these responsibilities he was aware that the pastoral care of the congregation was being neglected. He decided to appoint a chaplain to the cathedral, whose responsibility was to be 'vicar' to the regular congregation. I understand that the plan was worked out in principle without the congregation being told that the post might be filled by a woman.

I still think my appointment was a bold step. I was the first woman minister to join the staff of the cathedral. I later heard of one member of the congregation who, when she heard of my appointment, had serious doubts about whether she would be able to receive communion from me. Three months after I had been in post, she wondered what she had been worried about. One of the greatest compliments that I received was from someone who came regularly, although she was not very involved in the life of the cathedral. After she had experienced my ministry for about six months, she told me that when I went to the pulpit to preach she could now forget that I was a woman, and just listen to what I had to say. I was delighted. The word of God had become more important than the messenger. Apart from the reservation of the few, which I did not know about at the time, I was well received by both the staff and the congregation.

I had responsibility for overseeing all aspects of the congregational life of the cathedral. This included home study groups, young people and children's work, fellowship, pastoral care and outreach, together with a teaching and preaching ministry. Decisions about the life of the congregation were taken by the Congregational Committee which was the equivalent to a Parochial Church Council. At first, this was chaired by the provost, but later delegated to me as

cathedral chaplain. Some of the highlights of my time at
Bradford Cathedral were the twenty-four-hour conferences
with the Congregation Committee during which we worked
through important aspects of the ministry to the congregation.
One of the privileges I had concerned the cathedral verger
who was a committed Christian. Before working at the cathedral he had been a long-distance lorry driver. He told me
that although he was always pleased to show visitors around
the cathedral, he was also scared lest they ask him questions
about the Christian faith which he was unable to answer. He
longed to be able to talk about the gospel with some confidence. The result of this was that he joined a small evangelistic training programme that I was running and developed
a natural ability to gossip the gospel. A few years later he left
the cathedral to train with the Church Army and is now back
in Bradford serving as a Church Army evangelist.

I spent nearly five years at Bradford Cathedral. The job was
demanding and stimulating, but cathedrals are not the
easiest places in which to work, and, in my opinion, five
years is long enough for anyone to spend in such an environment! However, the same question presented itself to me as
had five years previously. Where do I go from here?
   Again I applied for numerous jobs; again I thought about
joining the Methodists, and actually walked to the nearby
Methodist church and knocked on the minister's door. In the
providence of God, he was out, and I never got around to
making an appointment. The Bishop of Bradford did suggest
that I look at an assistant curate's post in the diocese which I
very nearly accepted. I was not wholly convinced that it was
right, but there seemed to be nothing else. I was on the point
of accepting when three senior clergymen of the diocese, who
knew both me and the parish concerned, each approached
me independently and told me quite clearly that it was not
the right job for me. As God had sent three messengers with
the same words, I got the message and waited for further
instructions!
   The Church of England has a central agency called the

Clergy Appointments Adviser who makes known vacant posts and clergy looking for a move, and my name was put on to his list. It was through this means that I received an invitation from a church in Rochester diocese to consider working on a large housing estate in the parish of South Gillingham. This very large parish had four congregations served by three full-time clergy. I was asked to become the minister responsible for St Paul's Church on Parkwood. Parkwood was the largest private housing estate in Europe with a population of 10–12,000. It was the largest of the four areas of the parish but had no Anglican church building. The congregation had been in existence for about ten years when I joined them, and at that time consisted of about twelve families who attended fairly regularly. My brief was to build up the church on the estate. The base of operation was two terraced houses, one the minister's house and the other the 'Church House'. In this house the garage and front-room on the ground floor had been converted into a chapel which seated about thirty people. On paper, this was not the sort of job I was looking for, but I began to see that it would offer me a new challenge, so at the end of 1985 I moved from caring for a congregation of several hundred to one which scarcely numbered twenty on most Sundays.

The parish was run as if it were a team ministry, although it did not have that legal status. The vicar was a good team leader and allowed me to develop my own ministry, while being part of the team. My job description also included responsibility for adult education across the whole parish, so I found myself in a new but stimulating situation. Soon after I arrived, I was asked by the bishop to take over responsibility for reader training in the diocese, alongside my work in the parish. This I did for two years; it was probably very important for me at the time as it gave me further responsibility and was demanding in a different way from the routine work of the parish. It also enabled me to learn more about the diocese and to meet people throughout the whole area.

In 1987 the Church of England passed legislation permitting

women to become deacons. The diaconate is the first of the
three orders of bishop, priest and deacon. This was a significant step because it meant that for the first time women
could enter Holy Orders, and as such be entitled to be called
'Reverend'. Those of us who were deaconesses at the time
were permitted, if we wished, to be ordained deacon. For
many this was the cause of great rejoicing. Large celebra-
tions were planned for the first ordination of women to the
diaconate. My own feelings were very different. I had seen
myself, for many years, as not only a deacon, but as a full
member of the clergy team. I knew that, technically, I was
not a priest and respected the restrictions that were laid
upon me. I worked within those limitations but, for the most
part, what I did was the same as my clergy colleagues. The
churches in which I had worked had for many years ceased
to talk about 'the clergy' but rather about the 'church staff',
of which I was one. They treated me as if I were already
ordained. The congregation at Parkwood, for which I was
responsible, spoke of me as their vicar. Indeed, on one
occasion, one member introduced me to her friends as 'our
priest'. I therefore found it quite hard when asked in the
ordination service if I felt called to be a deacon in the church
of God. I wanted to reply, 'Yes, I did ten years ago, but I've
developed into a role more akin to that of a priest in the
intervening years.' For me, being made a deacon was not a
great occasion. It was a very painful and humiliating event.
It did not seem to mark a change for me personally. Rather I
felt that it was the church that had changed, and was
beginning to catch up with where I had been some years
previously. I would have preferred to have been made a
deacon in a private service with only the necessary witnesses
present. I thought that Ash Wednesday would have been a
suitable occasion as a penitential act on behalf of the church
for ignoring the diaconal ministry of women for so long. In
fact, I was ordained deacon in Rochester Cathedral in a
large service with many other deaconesses. Somehow, I got
through the service without dissolving into tears.

Being a deacon, rather than a deaconess, had one practical effect. Deacons, because they are clergy in the Church of England, are by virtue of this registrars and can conduct marriage services. As I was on the staff of a very large parish, I soon found myself taking weddings. Within three-and-a-half years, I had married nearly 100 couples.

Apart from weddings, the actual work that I did as a deacon was no different from what I had done as a deaconess. For that matter, it was not very different from what I had done initially as a parish worker; it was only my experience over the years that had changed my role. I had, by now, had hands laid on me three times. I was commissioned as a parish worker, ten years later made a deaconess, and about ten years after that made a deacon, yet I was still not a 'proper vicar' and still could not preside at the Communion Service, or be appointed as vicar of a parish. There were times when this was frustrating. It was certainly inconvenient, and most of the time seemed to me and to those among whom I worked to be sheer nonsense. I was, of course, very well aware of all the theological arguments and knew that this was more than just a pragmatic issue. The fact was that I had to live with the situation every day of my ministry. In practice, I found that the job was very demanding and offered tremendous opportunities. I was so grateful to be doing something that I enjoyed and found fulfilling.

Although becoming deacons did not greatly affect the actual work that we did, it did have an enormous psychological effect. This was much greater than I had expected. Once women were clergy, they began to be taken much more seriously, certainly by male clergy, which is a sad reflection on lay ministry.

Being a deacon had one very significant effect for me, in that it led to my being appointed Rural Dean of Gillingham. I was the first woman in the Church of England to hold that position. This would not have been possible had I remained a deaconess. My appointment happened in this way. Once the bishop had received the resignation from the outgoing rural dean, he wrote to all the incumbents asking for two names from among the clergy in the deanery whom they considered suitable to be the next rural dean. I was not asked because I was not an incumbent. Gillingham is a small deanery, having only eight incumbents, and as the outgoing rural dean was not consulted, seven replies were received. I understand that of these seven, five had mentioned my name. Discussions were held at the bishop's staff meeting, and the lawyers were consulted. They advised the bishop that it was legally possible for a deacon to be a rural dean. (Later when this was raised in the Legal Commission, the lawyers did not come to a common mind.) In due course, I received a letter from the bishop inviting me to accept his appointment. I held the post of rural dean for two-and-a-half years, and relinquished it reluctantly when appointed to a new post outside the deanery. I enjoyed the role very much indeed. To be a rural dean is to have some pastoral care for the clergy in the deanery and to be a link between the parishes and the bishop. As I had been appointed at the suggestion of the clergy in the deanery, they supported me and accepted me in that role from the very beginning. I didn't face any particular problems because I was a woman or because I was a deacon. I could not help with communion services during interregna or holiday periods, but I wouldn't have been able to do that very often even if I had been a priest because of the demands of my own parish. I did ensure that services were covered. Six out of the eight parishes had an interregnum during the time I was rural dean, so I became quite familiar with the procedures. I enjoyed working with the churchwardens and other lay leaders and assistant clergy during those times. My own incumbent left while I was rural dean. When his successor was appointed, I had the unusual experience of acting on behalf of the patron and presenting my own incumbent to the bishop at the Institution Service. It was to the credit of my previous and new incumbents that neither had any difficulty in accepting me as their rural dean. In deanery matters I had the main responsibility, and in parish matters the incumbent responsibility. It may sound impossible in theory, but in practice it worked very well indeed.

When the legislation was passed allowing women to be ordained deacon, a temporary procedure allowed them to be represented on General Synod in a special constituency, as part of the House of Clergy. In that election I was returned to synod by the Deacons of Canterbury Province. I had refused to stand for the House of Laity in the 1985 elections. I felt that as a deaconess I did not fairly represent lay people. I declared that I would not stand again until I could do so as an honest woman. The opportunity came in 1987, and again in 1990, when I was elected to represent the clergy of Rochester diocese.

By virtue of being returned to synod in 1987, I was invited to join the Advisory Council for the Church's Ministry (ACCM). This is the central body that advises the bishops of the Church of England on matters concerning the ordained and accredited ministry of the church. It is an area of interest that I had had for many years, and indeed I have previously been a member of one of ACCM's sub-committees, the Committee for Theological Education. Being a member of ACCM led in turn to being asked to chair a working party which was set up at the end of 1989 to consider the effect of making women deacons. It was interesting for me to have access to responses from the dioceses and to try and put together some guidelines for the deployment of deacons who are women. We became increasingly aware that we were, in fact, dealing with two issues: the diaconate and femininity. For several years now the subject of a permanent diaconate has been discussed but no concensus reached. Although the church now has, in effect, a permanent diaconate in its women, there is still no common mind on the theology or practice of this Order. The Church of England has much thinking to do on the subject of women in ordained ministry.

I worked for nearly five years on the Parkwood Estate. During this time the need for a church building became more evident and eventually, after much prayer and considerable negotiation by the diocese, a site in the centre of the estate was acquired and plans for a new church building put in hand. By this time a new incumbent had been appointed, and a pastoral scheme to set up a legal team ministry came into effect. The curate had left, and we were seeking to appoint our first vicar in the team. I was to fulfil the role of the other vicar, so it looked as if a new exciting phase was about to start.

Then came a summons from the bishop. Wondering what I had done wrong, I presented myself as requested. He told me, that in order to ease his work load, he was to appoint a personal residential chaplain, and he asked me to consider this post. After much heart searching, I accepted. It was a big decision to leave parochial ministry which I had enjoyed so much. It was also ironical that it was when I was happy in my ministry and intending to stay for several more years that the offer came to me. This was one reason why I considered it so carefully, for I knew from experience that posts of responsibility for women who are deacons are not offered very often.

I have only just started in this new work as assistant to the Bishop of Rochester, so cannot yet write from experience. As it is a new post I have no precedent to follow. It includes being the bishop's press officer, but excludes any liturgical responsibilities. Alongside the post of Bishop's Personal Chaplain, I have been appointed as Diocesan Deacon and Associate Diocesan Director of Ordinands. This includes pastoral oversight of women who are deacons and helping those who are exploring a vocation to the diaconate. In this new role, I am part of the bishop's senior staff and so present at his staff meetings.

As I look back over twenty-five years in the ministry of the church, I realise how far the ministry of women has developed. For me they have been exciting and fulfilling years, although not always easy. I have been privileged to be active while many changes have taken place, and have sometimes been in pioneer situations. The next ten years will also be very significant for women in the ministry of the Church of England. I hope to be able to play my part in that and help not only with the thinking and praying, but especially by getting on with the job to which I believe God has called me.

Postscript—a Personal View

by

Susan Penfold

Susan Penfold is a non-stipendiary deacon in the parish of Cononley with Bradley, North Yorkshire, where her husband Colin is Vicar

As I have worked through the varied contributions sent to me for this book, I have found myself wondering how the people who read the book will react to them. Will some of the things said be a surprise? Will it confirm some people's view that women should not be ordained? Or will it have the opposite effect? Will it leave some people thinking, 'Why a book on women in particular? Some of these stories could be told of men'? One reaction I would love to see would be if some people, women or men, whom God is calling to serve him in professional ministry, should get to the end and say, 'Perhaps I could see myself in that sort of role.'

My own reactions to the stories told here have been strongly coloured by the fact that I too am a woman in ministry. There have been many times when I've found myself saying, 'Yes, that's just like what happened to me,' and that has been as true of the experiences of my Free Church sisters as it has of my colleagues in the Church of England. Having said that, there have also been one or two surprises.

I was interested by Rosemary Harrison's story of what happened to her after the birth of her first baby. When my first child was born I felt that people were treating me as no longer a minister, but 'just a mum' now, and it took me a while to get back to active ministry, a process complicated by changing parishes in the middle. I'm not sure why our experiences should have been so different, but it's possibly because we were in a multi-church parish, and I found myself worshipping in a different church from the ones I'd been most recently working in.

Another surprise was discovering that Viv Faull had asked to take part in the ordination service a year after she was made deaconess, when her male colleagues were being priested. When I got to that stage in my ministry, I desperately wanted not to be at that service—really to pretend it wasn't happening. But my husband, who had trained alongside me and was made deacon when I was made deaconess, was being priested then. A few days later a priest from a neighbouring parish said to me, 'I saw your face as you came up for communion, and I suddenly realised what we were doing.' I would count that one of the worst days of my life—there didn't seem to be any real difference in God's calling to each of us, but it felt as though the church was making a great fuss of Colin's ministry, while virtually ignoring mine. Viv's story brought it all back, and I found myself nearly in tears over her manuscript.

One thing I hadn't realised is just how quickly things have changed for women ministers—certainly in the Church of England. I hadn't realised until I read Mavis Bexon's and Judith Rose's chapters just what conditions of work, especially housing and pay, were like for women twenty-five years ago, nor how much they were discriminated against in church structures. Of course I knew that as accredited lay workers or deaconesses they were technically lay people rather than clergy, but I hadn't realised what this would mean in terms of the acknowledgement (or otherwise) by the diocese, or their being excluded from clergy gatherings. Things were very different by the time I was made a deaconess in 1984. In a way I feel very thankful not to have had to fight those battles—being a pioneer can be a costly business. Like Viv Faull, I was the first woman in a previously all-male theological college, though I started training two years after Viv, and that year all but one of the

Church of England colleges were mixed. Things had changed very quickly indeed for women.

Pondering on the book as it has turned out, I feel sorry that I didn't manage to find a Free Church minister with longer experience of ministry, to see how things have changed there. (I did ask one, but she was too busy moving house for her retirement!) One thing that is clear from the Free Church contributors is that even when ordination is technically open to women, it doesn't follow that they will necessarily receive encouragement in that direction, nor that they won't encounter obstacles to their ministry because they are women. Sex discrimination still flourishes even when it has been officially abolished, as most women know only too well from their experience in the secular world! I find myself wondering whether in some ways the overt discrimination of the Church of England in not ordaining women to the priesthood might not be easier to cope with than the 'hidden' discrimination so many women experience—for example when Jane Hassell was told that some Baptist churches are reluctant to call women pastors, or Rose Barrett's feelings that the church expects a woman to put up with worse living conditions than a family man. (I suspect a single man might get a similarly rough deal in housing—though there'd probably be more volunteers to do his laundry!) So often men and women are declared equal in theory but treated differently in practice.

I also find myself sharing Rose Barrett's irritation at being part of a group addressed as 'Gentlemen'. When I first started at theological college, it took people a while to get used to my presence, but the announcements for 'first year men' were fairly quickly replaced by notices for 'students'. My immediate reaction is to want to put up my hand and say, 'Please can I come too?'—and occasionally I've done it. I had the experience again fairly recently in a vestry of clergy assembled for a confirmation service, although I suppose I was technically invisible on that occasion, as I was standing behind the clergyman who made the announcement. I'm afraid that being told that I'm an 'honorary gentleman' only adds insult to injury. I like being a woman!

One of the questions I've pondered as I've read these stories is whether women minister differently to men. Di Williams suggests there might be a difference when she talks about 'a powerful innate urge . . . to create and to nurture', which she sees 'as being bound up with being a woman'—though how much of this is about Di herself, and how much is it generally applicable to women? Both Rose Barrett and Jane Hassell would deny there is a specifically female style of working. Differences of approach have more to do with personality or theology. I think I would agree with that viewpoint, but I would want to add that both our family circumstances and our experience of life will affect the way we minister. Pastoral relationships are obviously different when people see you at toddler group or the school gate with your own children! And when preparing families for baptism, suggestions that they should try taking their children to church carry more weight when they know you face the weekly struggle of getting two children out of the house on time and persuading them to behave acceptably during the service, and do it singlehanded more often than not, because Sunday is Daddy's busy day! Of course men's ministry too is strongly influenced by their family circumstances, but on the whole people don't seem to react as strongly to this—somehow it seems to be more significant to be a mum than a dad.

On the whole the question of integrating family life and ministry seems to be more of an issue for women than men, mostly I suspect because women are more likely to be seen as the primary care-giver when it comes to rearing children. We may be happy to go along with that view, because it works well for our particular family—as is clearly the case for Rosemary Harrison and her family. But it isn't the only way to run a family, and I can sympathise with Teresa Rutterford for feeling so battered when people reacted against a different way of sharing family responsibilities. It doesn't seem right that the powers-that-be should be so much more concerned about a woman's family responsibilities than a man's. But I wonder whether this is an area where men suffer more discrimination than women—or rather their families suffer. I recently heard a clergyman's daughter saying that as a teenager she would have seen more of her father if her parents had been divorced and had to make proper arrangements for access.

My own feeling is that those of us who do struggle with the balance between family and ministry may have something powerful to offer the church—and we should be grateful that in some ways it is easier for us as women, because our congregations are often more understanding of the situation when we feel the need to give priority to our families than they are when men try to do the same. But because it is easier for us as women, we should try to avoid the trap of colluding with the stereotype that says that women are the main caregiver—if only so that our children can grow up knowing that there are other ways to run a family than mostly having Mum around, and also that they have the chance to form good relationships with both parents.

There are of course other areas where people perceive women differently from men. Judith Rose, Teresa Rutterford and Rose Barrett all raised the issue of how people react to women seeking to follow God's call to exercise leadership in the church. Why does it seem odd for women to look for more responsible jobs, but natural for men to do so? And why should a woman be described as having a 'Thatcherite style' while men have 'leadership potential'? Clearly there are still strong expectations among our congregations that women and men will function differently, but this seems to create a stereotype of 'woman' that fits uneasily on many women ministers. I don't suppose this problem is confined to the church, but hopefully people's perceptions will eventually change as they become more accustomed to seeing women in positions of authority, and perhaps describing it will help some people to see that the problem exists!

One of my aims in producing this book was to give as broad a picture as possible of women in professional ministry—and within that I had hoped to include the story of someone who was opposed to the ordination of women, but prepared to work in an 'assistant' capacity. I had assumed that there were such women, at least within the Church of England, where even if they weren't ordained deacon, they would be deaconesses or accredited lay workers. What took me by surprise was how difficult it was to find such women. They do indeed exist, but they are very few and far between—and it proved impossible to persuade one to write for the book. As I made enquiries I discovered that this too was something that had changed over the last few years. Mavis Bexon told me that she and many of her colleagues had started out in ministry opposed to the ordination of women to the priesthood, but their experience over the years had brought them to a different opinion (Judith Rose writes about that in her chapter). For many women in ministry, as in Jane Hassell's account, the tension between God's call (and indeed the jobs they find themselves doing) and a theology which opposes the ordination of women seems to lead to a radical change of views—though hopefully that is reinforced by a careful study of Scripture, otherwise we could all be deluding ourselves.

But even if people agree that women could be ordained, there is still the question of who should be ordained—and I realise there are far more theologies of ordination than there are denominations represented in this book! Chris Howden isn't ordained, but is fulfilling a remarkably similar role to many non-stipendiary women deacons in the Church of England. We would probably do more work with funerals and baptism enquiries, but that would be true of the Church of England generally as compared with a Baptist church. Her chapter raises interesting questions about the recognition we give to people's ministries if they don't have the title 'Rev'.

My strongest reaction to the accounts in this book has been of gratitude; gratitude to God for giving such gifts to women, and gratitude to these women for being prepared to share themselves in print. One aspect of the debate over women's roles in the church (including the ordination debate in the Church of England) which has bothered me very much is the message it seems to be giving to women outside, or on the fringes of the church. One incident I will never forget is sitting in my room at theological college in Cambridge with an undergraduate who was thinking very seriously indeed about the Christian faith. 'I could never become a Christian,' she said, 'because of the way the church treats women.' I could have tackled questions like the resurrection or the Trinity—or even made a stab at the problem of suffering— but this one made me feel sick inside, and I really didn't know how to reply. It's an objection with a great deal of force to it. My only answer is that God loves women very much indeed—and that Jesus treated women with the utmost respect in sharp contrast to the prevailing attitudes of his society. But it's not easy for women to believe that when they don't always see it acted out in the life of the church.

Since then I have encountered the same objection from women in many different forms—though never expressed as clearly as that. And I have met Christian parents whose daughters have left the church because they perceive it to be a place where they will suffer discrimination. That frightens me very much, because I too have a daughter. She's only four now, but what of the future? Last year she played at being a bishop, happily unaware that she could never be one as things stand at the moment. What will happen when she finds out? Will she perceive it as a message that God loves her brother more than her? I would see every woman called by God and exercising her ministry in the church (in whatever form) as a sign that God loves women just as much as men—that we live in God's 'New Age' (to quote Jane Hassell), where there is no distinction between men and women, but we are all one in our union with Christ Jesus.